HIDDEN HISTORY
of
ALABAMA AVIATION

HIDDEN HISTORY
of
ALABAMA AVIATION

Billy J. Singleton

THE
History
PRESS

Published by The History Press
Charleston, SC
www.historypress.com

Copyright © 2024 by Billy Singleton
All rights reserved

Cover images courtesy of the University of New Mexico Libraries, University of Texas and Gadsden Public Library.

Images not credited are courtesy of the author.

First published 2024

Manufactured in the United States

ISBN 9781467156264

Library of Congress Control Number: 2023948361

For those Alabama aviators whose stories are hidden within the pages of history.

CONTENTS

PREFACE

The history of aviation in Alabama is a remarkable and compelling narrative that begins with early visionaries who dreamed of building flying machines decades before the first successful flights of Orville and Wilbur Wright. The subsequent growth and development of the aviation and aerospace industry in Alabama would encompass the establishment of the Air University of the United States Air Force at Montgomery; the Marshall Space Flight Center in Huntsville, responsible for the design and development of the Saturn V rocket that propelled humans to the moon; and the Airbus U.S. Manufacturing Facility in Mobile, which assembles more than one hundred aircraft annually for delivery to airlines around the world. Although the state of Ohio claims the distinction of being the birthplace of aviation and North Carolina first in flight, Alabama is where aviation and aerospace spread its wings.

Often overlooked in the historical narrative of aviation in Alabama are lesser-known stories relating to individuals and events that have been consigned to the footnotes of history. *Hidden History of Alabama Aviation* is a collection of stories that fill the gaps between the documented elements of aviation history—stories so interesting and unique that it is impossible to simply dismiss them as fragments of aviation trivia.

Many of the stories included in *Hidden History of Alabama Aviation* can be attributed to Asa Rountree Jr. (1896–1983). His forty-six-year tenure as the first and longest-serving director of aeronautics is meticulously documented through his collection of personal papers preserved in the Alabama

Department of Archives and History. These files include handwritten notes intended for use as an outline for a book on the history of aviation in Alabama. Although the project never materialized, his notes are an invaluable resource in preserving this important facet of our history.

The stories included in this work are often heroic, sometimes humorous and occasionally tragic but always interesting and entertaining. It is important to consider that these stories describe events that often defined the careers, if not the lives, of the individuals involved. Even though their names may not be memorialized in recorded histories, each deserves to be remembered for his or her dedication, achievements and experiences that are essential in telling the story of aviation in Alabama.

ACKNOWLEDGEMENTS

The author is deeply indebted to the following individuals and organizations for their contributions and support of this project: the Alabama Department of Archives and History (ADAH); the Air Force Historical Research Agency, Maxwell Air Force Base, Alabama (AFHRA); Alabama Aviation Hall of Fame (AAHOF); Special Collections, Center for Southwest Research, University of New Mexico Libraries (UNM Libraries); John L. Marty Jr.; Craig Scott, Gadsden Public Library; Carey Heatherly, Archivist, University of Montevallo; Air University Office of History, Maxwell Air Force Base; the National Museum of Naval Aviation; Wright State University Special Collections and Archives; American Heritage Center, University of Wyoming; and Bob Peck, Historic Mobile Preservation Society.

The author gratefully acknowledges the contributions of Rebecca Todd Minder, director, and Dr. Susan Reynolds, editor, of *Alabama Heritage* magazine for their many contributions to preserving the history of aviation in Alabama.

The author is especially grateful to Joe Gartrell, acquisitions editor; Ryan Finn, senior production editor; and the staff of The History Press for their guidance, suggestions and contributions in making this project a reality.

INTRODUCTION

The month of October 1949 represents a milestone in the history of aviation in Alabama, as the state crossed the threshold into a new age with the relocation of the Army Ordinance Research and Development Division Sub-Office (Rocket) from Fort Bliss, Texas, to Redstone Arsenal in Huntsville. Tasked with the development of the guided missile program for the United States military, Wernher von Braun and his team of scientists propelled the city of Huntsville and the state of Alabama into the global race for space—a competition that would redefine the legacy of aviation in Alabama and create the foundation for development of the aerospace industry in the state.

Prior to the emergence of the era of rocketry, the people of Alabama eagerly embraced aviation. Even though early visionaries in Alabama pursued the development of a flying machine during the late nineteenth century, the airplane first arrived in the state on March 26, 1910, when Orville Wright ascended in a Wright Flyer above the expanse of cotton fields near Montgomery. The flight was conducted in conjunction with the establishment of the nation's first civilian flying school and represents the first powered, controlled and sustained flight of a heavier-than-air machine over Alabama.

The arrival of the flying machine and the need to train aviators set a precedent for the future. Enrolled at the Wright School at Montgomery, Walter Richard Brookins became the first student aviator to be trained in the state. Although the Wright brothers believed that their invention would

On March 26, 1910, Orville Wright completed the first flight of a heavier-than-air flying machine over Alabama. *Wright State University Special Collections and Archives.*

make future wars practically impossible, the genial climate and suitable terrain that attracted them to Alabama convinced officials of the Army Air Service to establish an aviation training field in the Pike Road community to train aviators for service in Europe during the First World War.

Military flight training became a dominant factor in the history of aviation in Alabama. As the clouds of a second global conflict gathered over Europe in 1939, President Franklin Roosevelt unleashed the industrial might of the United States to become the great arsenal of democracy to oppose the Axis Powers of Germany, Italy and Japan. Before the end of the Second World War, only Texas and Florida rivalled the state of Alabama in the training of military aviators. Today, the legacy of military aviation education and training continues to be a dominant influence in Alabama through the Air University at Maxwell Air Force Base and Fort Novesel, the home of Army Aviation at Ozark.

Between wars, Alabama aviators achieved international acclaim for their daring exploits during the Golden Age of Aviation. Milton "Skeets" Elliott of Gadsden earned a reputation as one of the most celebrated motion picture and stunt pilots in the United States. Ruth Elder of Anniston earned her place in aviation history as the first female aviator to attempt to cross the Atlantic Ocean by airplane. John Edward Long Jr., who began his flying career in 1932, is recognized by the Guinness Book of World Records as having accumulated more time as a pilot than any individual in the history of aviation.

Intermingled among the narratives of the notable aviators and events that define the history of aviation in Alabama are lesser known but equally important stories that have not received widespread attention. In May 1940, First Lady of the United States Eleanor Roosevelt accompanied Charles Alfred "Chief" Anderson, considered the "Father of Black Aviation," on an aerial tour over the Tuskegee Institute campus in a two-seat Piper J-3 Cub civilian training aircraft despite the strong objections of her protective detail. In July 1948, an encounter between the pilots of an Eastern Air Lines aircraft and an unidentified flying object in the predawn hours over Montgomery became the catalyst for an official investigation of this phenomenon by the U.S. Air Force. In Montevallo, the administrators of Alabama College pursued the construction of an airport to finance a gymnasium that could not be obtained by other means.

These unique and unusual stories chronicle the people and events that have been hidden within the historical narrative of aviation in Alabama. The preservation of these stories is essential in establishing an accurate record of the state's diverse aviation heritage and affording future generations the opportunity to understand and appreciate the people and events that have contributed to the remarkable legacy of aviation in Alabama.

THE PIONEERS

The story of aviation in Alabama is a remarkable saga that began decades before the first successful flight of a heavier-than-air machine by Orville and Wilbur Wright and includes many unprecedented events unique in the chronicles of powered flight.

DREAMS OF FLYING MACHINES

The Wright brothers were not the first humans to fly, nor did they claim to be the first. In an article published in December 1913 titled "How We Made the First Flight," Orville Wright recalled their historic achievement:

> *The Flight lasted only twelve seconds, but it was nevertheless the first time in the history of the world in which a machine that carried a man had raised itself by its own power into the air in full flight, had sailed forward without a reduction in speed, and had finally landed at a point as high as that from which it started.*

Even though ascensions of lighter-than-air balloons had previously thrilled crowds at local fairs in Alabama, the first documented powered, controlled and sustained flight of a heavier-than-air machine over the state occurred on March 26, 1910, when Orville Wright ascended above the cotton fields west of Montgomery. The flight was made in conjunction with the establishment of the nation's first civilian flying school to train aviators for the recently

A marker located near the Suggsville community in Clarke County reads, "Site of extensive aviation experiments by Dr. Denny 100 years before the Wright Brothers."

formed Wright Exhibition Company. Although Orville Wright was the first to achieve sustained flight in a heavier-than-air machine over Alabama, he was not the first in the state to conceive of the possibility.

The earliest reference relating to aerial experiments in Alabama can be found about thirteen miles east of Grove Hill, the county seat of Clarke County, along a narrow two-lane blacktop road known locally as the Old Line Road. Traveling south, just beyond the point that the pavement ends, a granite marker erected by the Clarke County Historical Society commemorates the once thriving community of Suggsville. The narrative etched into the face of the marker proclaims, "Site of extensive aviation experiments by Dr. Denny 100 years before the Wright Brothers." This claim is based on the life of physician and naturalist Andrew Denny, who purportedly developed an interest in the construction of a flying machine.

A native of Boston, Massachusetts, Andrew Denny relocated to Clarke County in 1836 following graduation from Harvard Medical School. At Suggsville, Denny established a reputation as a noted physician who was employed in treating the most dangerous and unusual cases. He was also considered to be a peculiar individual who endeavored to construct a flying machine.

Even though Denny was viewed as being somewhat eccentric by the residents of Suggsville, other acquaintances preferred to describe him as a visionary, a term applied to other early aerial experimenters in Alabama. Denny has been described as a man of multiple interests who maintained nearly two thousand hives of bees. Friends and neighbors observed Denny sitting for hours closely studying the insects in flight. Local historians suggest that his interest in bees may have been the catalyst that convinced Denny to pursue development of a flying machine designed to remain aloft by a mechanical flapping of the wings, a concept known as an ornithopter. Denny invested $8,000 (equivalent to about $200,000 in 2023) in his quest to replicate the natural ability of bees to sustain flight.

Although Andrew Denny is reputed to be the first aerial experimenter in Alabama, it should be noted that he did not begin conducting experiments until arriving in Suggsville in 1836, and these efforts may not have been initiated until 1860, twenty-four years later. Considering that Orville and Wilbur Wright began their experiments in 1899, the claim that Andrew Denny preceded the efforts of the Wrights by one hundred years is not based in fact.

Two years after Andrew Denny arrived in Suggsville to begin his endeavors to develop a flying machine, Lewis Archer Boswell was born in Lunenburg County, Virginia. Like Denny, Boswell was a man of medicine, graduating from the University of Virginia before enrolling at the Jefferson Medical College in Philadelphia. After finishing a special course of study at Johns Hopkins School of Medicine in Baltimore, Louis Boswell relocated to Greenwood, Mississippi, to establish a medical practice. In addition to medicine, Boswell developed a passion for ornithology, a branch of zoology relating to the study of birds. This passion would become the stimulus in convincing Boswell of the feasibility of a functional flying machine.

In 1869, Boswell married and moved to the Red Hill Plantation in Talladega County, Alabama. During the next five years, Boswell continued his study of the concept of a flying machine. In April 1874, he applied to the U.S. Patent Office for his "Improvements in Aerial Propeller Wheels," a design developed to propel a flying machine through the air. He employed a jeweler in Talladega to construct a miniature model of his aerial boat, which utilized his propeller wheel design. The model measured about twelve inches in length and was powered by a clock-spring mechanism. According to recollections of family members, Boswell would place the model on a table, start it and watch as it sailed across the room. The patent for his aerial propeller wheels was granted in September 1874.

It is important to note that patent applications of this period were based on prophetic concepts. A pioneer patent did not require a working model, only a description of predicted results rather than those achieved. The experimenter needed only to describe how to construct and use the device. A functioning prototype was not a requirement of the patent application during this era.

Boswell spent his remaining years soliciting financing to develop a lightweight motor to provide propulsion for his design. In 1900, he contacted Secretary of War Elihu Root, requesting a loan of $1,000 for this purpose. In his letter, Boswell stated, "You need a flying machine, I claim to have contrived all needful devices to ascend and descend at will, with ease and safety, and to guide right and left as readily as one does a canoe on a still lake." The Board of Ordnance and Fortification respectfully declined his request because of its financial support of experiments in air navigation being conducted by Samuel Langley of the Smithsonian Institution.

Boswell's claim to have contrived all necessary devices to ascend and descend at will may have been related to his September 1901 application to the U.S. Patent Office for a "Steering Mechanism for Dirigible Airships." The design incorporated a three-axis control of pitch (nose of the machine up and down), roll (movement of the wings to turn the machine) and yaw (nose right and left). Although the patent, approved in May 1903, did specify a control system for dirigible airships, it appears to have been his intent to combine the aerial propeller wheels and steering mechanism designs to construct a flying machine.

Following Boswell's death in November 1909, a group of citizens of Talladega began promoting the belief that he had flown a machine of his design prior to the historic flight of the Wright brothers. The catalyst for this belief was an article published in a July 1925 edition of the *Birmingham News*. The article included a photograph supposedly of the Boswell machine, known as the *Missionary*, in flight over rural Calhoun County. The caption accompanying the photograph informed readers that the first flight made by a heavier-than-air machine was reported to have taken place in November 1902 at Anniston, Alabama.

However, according to Boswell's daughter, the photographic image was artificially produced to solicit funds for his experiments. Although stories by those who claim to have known someone who observed Boswell operate his

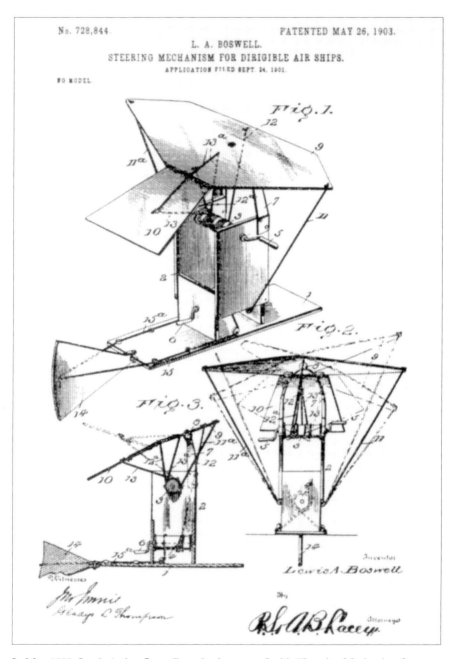

In May 1903, Lewis Archer Boswell received a patent for his "Steering Mechanism for Dirigible Airships." *U.S. Patent and Trademark Office.*

machine continued to persist, his daughter stated that her father spent most of his life studying the possibility of heavier-than-air flight and was always making experiments, but he never flew.

Even though Boswell became the first experimenter in Alabama to receive a patent relating to the development of a flying machine, there is no evidence to indicate that any of his designs advanced beyond the conceptual stage of development. The distinction of being the first experimenter in Alabama to construct a flying machine prototype would be earned by a watchmaker and street preacher residing in the port city of Mobile.

Born in Saltillo, Mississippi, in 1862, John Ellis Fowler relocated to Mobile in 1884 and established a clock and sewing machine repair business in a small shop on Dauphin Street. Fowler was a well-known character in Mobile for two reasons: his extraordinary mechanical ability and his activities as a street evangelist who spread the gospel from atop a produce box at the corner of Dauphin and Royal Streets. He also earned the reputation of being an aerial experimenter and inventor who developed an interest in the design and construction of flying machines.

Before his death in 1939, Fowler designed three flying machine prototypes. Unlike those of other visionaries in Alabama, photographic evidence exists of two of these designs, which were constructed behind a large wooden fence on the grounds of Monroe Park. To obtain financial support for his projects, Fowler charged an admission fee of ten cents for spectators to enter the enclosure to view the machine and listen to his theories relating to the design of flying machines. To encourage donations, Fowler always insisted that the funds would be used to make good headway to finish the machine.

The first of these designs provided for a cane chair to accommodate upright seating for the aviator. The machine sat on an undercarriage consisting of four bicycle-type wheels to be utilized for taking off and landing on the soft grass of Monroe Park. The monoplane design, circa 1902, consisted of one large lifting surface supplemented by a second horizontal plane at the rear of the machine. Fowler used his expertise in clock repair to design a mechanism that rotated two propellers at a high rate of speed to propel the machine through the air.

Fowler's second flying machine to be constructed at Monroe Park was designed to take off and land from either the ground or water. The marine hull included retractable landing gear for launching and landing the machine on a firm surface. In flight, the craft was supported by three separate lifting surfaces—the bottom, intermediate and top planes. Diagonal surfaces were situated between the horizontal planes to increase the lifting force produced

John Ellis Fowler of Mobile was known for his extraordinary mechanical ability and interest in the design of a flying machine. *Historic Mobile Preservation Society, Minnie Mitchell.*

John Ellis Fowler constructed two prototypes of his flying machine designs at Monroe Park in Mobile. *Historic Mobile Preservation Society, Minnie Mitchell.*

by the three engines and propellers installed on each wing section. Fowler believed that these diagonal planes, once covered with fabric, would produce a strong lifting effect that would shorten the distance the machine traveled on the surface before taking to the air.

The complex design included a mechanism to allow the leading edges of the wings to be inclined upward to lift the nose of the machine into the air. Maneuvering to the right and left was achieved by mechanically rotating the wings in opposite directions. The rudder surface, hinged to allow lateral and vertical movement, was installed at the rear of the craft to assist in turns, climbs and descents. In June 1926, Joh Fowler received approval from the U.S. Patent Office for his flying machine design. Fowler was also awarded a patent for his "Propeller for Flying Machines" that provided for greater pulling effect achieved with less speed of the motor.

In a 1902 newspaper interview, Fowler invited the public to Monroe Park to see one of his machines fly. However, the large crowd that assembled to observe the demonstration returned home disappointed. For unexplained reasons, Fowler never removed his flying machine from inside the enclosure. A subsequent newspaper announcement stated that Fowler would instead make the machine move in midair the following Sunday. Depending on the news outlet reporting the event, the machine was either destroyed by anxious citizens fearful that Fowler would kill himself or by an unidentified group of men for reasons never explained.

As with other early experimenters, witnesses reported that Fowler achieved sustained flight in one of his designs. Fowler did eventually fly, but not in a machine of his own construction. In 1924, he was taken aloft in an airplane at the original Bates Field in Mobile, a short distance from the Monroe Park location where he previously displayed his flying machine designs. Fowler explained that he delayed taking a flight because he always wanted his first to be in a machine of his own design. Even though he enjoyed the flight, he stated that the experience did not give him any thrill. Following his death in October 1939, John Fowler was buried in an unmarked grave at Magnolia Cemetery in Mobile. In March 1997, the life of the inventor was commemorated by relatives and admirers with the placement of a headstone on his grave that proclaims "John Ellis Fowler, Pioneer of Flight."

Unlike Andrew Denny and Louis Archer Boswell, who obtained formal educations in the field of medicine, John Fowler was largely self-educated. During his years operating a watch and sewing machine repair business, Fowler developed strong innovative and mechanical skills that allowed him to transform his conceptual ideas into actual prototypes. Another aspiring

An astute observer of nature, William LaFayette Quick believed that he could design a flying machine to replicate the flight of buzzards. *AAHOF.*

experimenter, William Lafayette Quick, also lacked the benefit of a formal education. Like Fowler, Quick was considered an innovator by friends and acquaintances. He operated Quick's Mill at New Market, a community located about fifteen miles northwest of Huntsville. The mill consisted of a foundry, blacksmith forge, sawmill, cotton gin, gristmill and the first electric power generator in rural Madison County.

An experimenter and inventor, Quick received a patent in 1884 for an agricultural implement known as a hillside plow. An astute observer of nature, William Quick believed that he could construct a flying machine based on his study of the flight of buzzards. He began construction of his flying machine in 1900, a project that would require almost eight years to complete. Unlike the more common biplane configuration used during this period, Quick developed a monoplane with an identifiable fuselage to allow the operator to sit in an upright position. The machine included a harness-type mechanism to allow the operator to control the up and down movement of the machine. Leaning forward, the operator could cause the nose of the machine to incline upward. Positioning the body aft produced the opposite effect. The Quick machine also utilized a tractor propulsion system instead of the more typical pusher systems used in other designs. Furthermore, instead of utilizing a landing skid, the landing gear on the Quick machine included two main wheels and a tailwheel.

Although no historical evidence exists to substantiate the event, family members relate that in 1908 Quick made one attempt to get his machine into the air. According to his eldest son, the machine was transported to a field on the Quick farm that had a slight incline before sloping gently downhill, terrain that Quick believed was well suited to aid in the production of lift. Because the engine lacked sufficient power to lift heavier weights, Quick's sixteen-year-old son, William Massey Quick, attempted to operate the machine. Once the engine was started, the machine began to roll slowly across the grass. Gaining speed, it reached the upsloping terrain, shivered like a kite and then lurched into the air. Years later, a family member estimated that the machine climbed to an altitude of eight to ten feet and traveled

The restored flying machine of William LaFayette Quick is displayed at the U.S. Space and Rocket Center in Huntsville.

about sixty to seventy-five feet before the left wing dropped, causing the machine to strike the ground.

Following this one attempt at flight, the machine was hauled to a nearby creek bed, where it remained for several years. Eventually, it was moved to a shed on the Quick farm. In 1964, local members of the Experimental Aircraft Association received permission to restore the machine. Following a four-year effort, the restored flying machine of William Quick was placed on display at Birmingham International Airport before being relocated for permanent display at the U.S. Space and Rocket Center in Huntsville.

Although Quick never attempted another flight with his invention, he continued his efforts to improve the design. In October 1913, he received a patent for his *Improved Flying Machine*. This design differed significantly from his earlier machine in that it included an improved pitch control mechanism, folding wings, and a retractable landing gear. In 1982, William Lafayette Quick was inducted into the Alabama Aviation Hall of Fame in recognition of his early aviation experiments.

In many respects, the story of aviation in Alabama began in rural Clarke County, where noted physician and aerial experimenter Andrew

Denny envisioned the possibility of applying the principals of nature to the construction of a flying machine. This dream was shared by other early experimenters who devoted their lives to the pursuit of human flight. For more than 150 years, aviation and aerospace have remained a source of inspiration and motivation for the people of Alabama. From early aerial experimenters to the race for space, the people of Alabama have demonstrated an enduring commitment to the growth and development of these vital industries, a commitment that will ensure the future of aviation and aerospace in the state.

WALTER BROOKINS: ALABAMA'S FIRST STUDENT PILOT

Credited with the first powered, controlled and sustained flight in a heavier-than-air machine over the sand dunes at Kitty Hawk, North Carolina, in December 1903, Orville and Wilbur Wright considered themselves the principal manufacturer of flying machines in the emerging aviation industry. By 1909, however, their dominance of aviation technology was being challenged by an increasing number of designers and aerial enthusiasts in the United States and abroad. To generate interest among potential customers and demonstrate the superiority of their flying machine design, the brothers formed a new business enterprise, the Wright Exhibition Company, to train a cadre of aviators to travel throughout the country to set new aviation records and fly for a fee at aeronautical exhibitions, county fairs and other large public gatherings.

Because harsh winter weather conditions in their native Ohio prevented the use of their flying field at Huffman Prairie for several months each year, the Wrights decided to take advantage of the genial climate and suitable terrain of the southern United States to establish a spring training camp for the student aviators. Requirements for the proposed site included a region having short winters, a mild climate and flat, unobstructed farmland—conditions considered favorable for the operation of their flying machine. In February 1910, Wilbur Wright left Ohio to begin a tour to investigate atmospheric and meteorological conditions and suitable landing sites in the Southeast. He visited Atlanta and Augusta, Georgia, but was unable to locate a site he deemed to be satisfactory. Wright then traveled to Jacksonville, Florida, where an acquaintance suggested he visit Montgomery, Alabama, a region known for its mild winter weather and abundance of flat farmland.

In Montgomery, Wright was taken on a tour of the city by members of the Commercial Club, a predecessor of the local chamber of commerce. After visiting several sites, he was shown a one-hundred-acre tract of land located three miles west of the city and owned by local merchant Frank Kohn. Wright inspected every inch of the property, paying close attention to even the smallest detail. He decided that it was just the class of property he had been seeking and was located far enough from the city to provide a degree of privacy.

Workers soon began transforming the former cotton field into Alabama's first flying field by cutting down trees and removing undergrowth. Initially, a few small trees and shrubs were left standing to beautify the area, but these were later removed at the request of Orville Wright so the area would be completely free of obstructions. An article in the *Montgomery Advertiser* newspaper reported that the field had been cleared of bushes and stretches over a great acreage clear of all encumbrances.

In March 1910, with preparations for the initiation of training complete, Wright then began the process of training five student pilots who would

The nation's first civilian flying school was established by Orville and Wilbur Wright in Montgomery. *Wright State University Special Collections and Archives.*

become the initial class of aviators of the Wright Exhibition Team. The first slated for training was Walter Richard Brookins of Dayton, Ohio. Under the tutelage of Orville Wright, Brookins first learned to manage the Flyer in the air. He practiced straight and level flight before being taught to maneuver the machine in a turn. Next he practiced taking the machine into the air and bringing it to earth again in proximity to the shed that was used for storage of the aircraft during periods of inclement weather. The training program at Montgomery was primitive, according to Brookins:

The machine that Orville taught me to fly was the same one that Wilbur flew in France. This airplane had been flown for quite a few hours and on one of our first flights the chain that ran from the wing warp control over the tin covered leading edge of the wing to the rear beam broke and we were without lateral control. But Orville, by his clever handling of the plane, avoiding a turn and going straight ahead, landed us safely about ten feet from a barbed wire fence. Now this chain was just an ordinary bathtub chain and the constant moving back and forth over the piece of tin on the leading edge of the wing had worn it knife edge thin before it broke. Right there we increased the factor of safety by replacing the bathtub chain with bicycle chain.

Because the airplane was still an unknown technology, having limited public applications, no federal guidelines relating to training or certification had been established by the federal government. Consequently, student aviators typically received training in becoming airborne, returning to earth, making a circuit of the field and landing the machine without power should the thirty-five-horsepower engine fail. Regarding his training, Brookins stated:

After I had approximately two hours and forty minutes of instruction in the air, Orville turned me loose on my first solo flight and to my consternation, the motor cut out and I had to make a forced landing which I did successfully thanks to the training I received from Orville who had been very painstaking in teaching me not only to fly, but the reason and theory of flying. After Orville once taught one something, it was so thoroughly explained and demonstrated that you never forgot it.

After his initial solo flight, Brookins began training to become what the Wright brothers described as a left-hand aviator. Normally, the Flyer was flown from the left-hand seat to offset the weight of the engine. Because the lever that operated the wing-warping, or lateral control system, was situated between the two seats, it was operated with the right hand. The flying instructor, seated in the right seat, manipulated the control with the left hand, hence the name. Becoming a left-hand aviator, Walter Brookins earned the distinction of not only being the first student pilot to be trained in Alabama but also the first flight instructor to be trained in state. During a speech at a Wright Celebration Dinner held in Dearborn, Michigan, in 1938, Brookins described his experiences teaching other students to operate the machine:

> *Several days after my solo flight, Mr. Wright was taking up a passenger and the plane on leaving the monorail flipped the carriage that carried the plane down the monorail into one of the propellers and broke the end off. As we had no other propellers available, Orville went back to Dayton to forward one and left me in charge of the school to teach students among whom was Archibald Hoxsey who later took up our former Pres. Theodore Roosevelt for his first flight in the air.*

After receiving a replacement propeller, strong winds prevented the operation of the Flyer for several days. Brookins and Hoxsey soon devised a plan to take advantage of the calm surface winds that existed after sunset. On May 25, 1910, the two aviators proceeded to launch the Flyer at approximately 10:30 p.m. in the stillness of the late evening and continued to conduct flights until dawn. These flights represent some of the earliest night operations in aviation history. Brookins recalled:

> *I completed the training of Hoxsey during the night the earth was supposed to pass through the tail of Halley's Comet. The weather and the light from a full southern moon were perfect and we made about a dozen flights that night. The next day Hoxsey soloed, and we then returned to Dayton where the Wrights set up a much bigger school.*

After the school closed in May 1910, Brookins returned to the Wright School at Huffman Prairie near Dayton to perfect his aviation skills before beginning his career as an exhibition pilot. Brookins and his fellow aviators were considered celebrities in cities and towns where they performed. In October 1910, Phil Parmelee, a member of the Wright Exhibition team, demonstrated a Wright machine at the Alabama State Fair in Birmingham.

Walter Richard Brookins (*right*) became the first student aviator in Alabama in March 1910 at the flying school of the Wright brothers in Montgomery.

Following his first solo flight, Walter Brookins (*left*) was selected to train fellow student Archibald Hoxsey in Montgomery. *Wright State University Special Collections and Archives.*

Walter Brookins soon emerged as the star of the team, setting world records for altitude, speed and cross-country flight. However, the exhibition business proved to be a hazardous endeavor. In October 1910, team member Ralph Johnstone was fatally injured in an accident in Denver, Colorado. Two months later, Archibald Hoxsey, one of the original Montgomery students, died in an accident in Los Angeles. Before the team disbanded in November 1911, five of the nine original aviators employed by the Wright brothers had lost their lives in accidents.

Walter Brookins, Alabama's first student pilot, passed away peacefully in April 1953 at Los Angeles, California. Fittingly, he was the first of many renowned aviators to be buried at the Portal of Folded Wings Shrine to Aviation at Valhalla Memorial Park in North Hollywood, California.

THE GREAT TRANSCONTINENTAL AIR RACE

During the decade that followed the first successful flight of a heavier-than-air machine by Orville and Wilbur Wright, aviation remained a pursuit reserved primarily for adventuresome, well-to-do sportsman. Use of the frail, unreliable aircraft was typically limited to publicity flights and exhibitions with intrepid aviators attempting to set altitude, speed and distance records during appearances at aviation meets, county fairs and large public gatherings.

In January 1910, the *Los Angeles Examiner* newspaper, owned by William Randolph Hearst, sponsored the Los Angeles International Air Meet. The event brought together the world's leading aviators and aircraft manufacturers for eleven days of competitions designed to promote and advance the field of aviation. Predictably, the aerial meet incorporated several publicity stunts, including the first delivery of a newspaper by airplane. Because of his position as sponsor of the event, Hearst was taken aloft in an airplane by the world-renowned aviator Louis Paulhan of France. Hearst became so enamored of the concept of the airplane that he announced sponsorship of a $50,000 prize for the first aviator to complete a transcontinental flight in an airplane within a period of thirty days or less.

Most aviators of the day, including Orville and Wilbur Wright, felt that such a lengthy journey would exceed the limits of current engine technology and the durability of the aircraft structure. Regardless of the concerns expressed by the Wrights, Calbraith Perry Rodgers and Robert Fowler, the only aviators to officially enter the competition, used flying machines constructed by the Wright brothers for their transcontinental attempts. Rodgers elected to begin his flight on September 17, 1911, departing Sheepshead Bay in New York bound for Pasadena, California, in the *Vin Fiz*, named for the grape-flavored soft drink produced by his sponsor, the Armour Meatpacking Company. Rodgers planned to follow a westerly route through the Midwest before proceeding south to avoid overflying the Rocky Mountains.

Unlike his competitor, Robert Fowler began his journey from San Francisco and proceeded east along a route across the southern United States to avoid the harsh winter weather conditions common in the northeast section of the country. Fowler's route of flight would take him from San Francisco over Arizona, New Mexico and Fort Worth, Texas, before crossing the states of Louisiana, Mississippi, Alabama, Georgia and Florida. Fowler believed that he could make the flight in twenty days. He added ten days to the schedule to allow time for rest, maintenance of his aircraft and inclement weather, a timetable that would allow him to complete the flight within the required thirty-day period.

After purchasing a Model B Flyer from Orville and Wilbur Wright, Fowler received instructions from the famous brothers in the care and operation of the machine. Sponsored by the Cole Motor Company of Indianapolis, Indiana, Fowler christened his machine the *Cole Flyer*. After he completed training at the Wright School in Dayton, Ohio, the *Cole Flyer* was transported to San Francisco by rail.

In an age that preceded the introduction of even the most basic forms of aerial navigation, Fowler planned to use the only reliable system for cross-country navigation available: the transcontinental railroads tracks, which he referred to as the "iron compass." In addition to providing a visual aid, the railroad provided an additional advantage of having a support crew transported by rail readily available along the route of flight. The Cole Motor Company arranged for a train car branded the *Fowler Special* to be loaded with fuel, water and spare parts. To assist in keeping Fowler in shape, boxing trainer Tim McGrath would accompany the *Fowler Special* to ensure that the aviator maintained a proper diet and sleep schedule and to control Fowler's exposure to curious onlookers at the various stopping points.

More than ten thousand spectators gathered on September 11, 1911, to watch Fowler take off from Golden Gate Park in San Francisco. From the outset, the flight was filled with almost insurmountable challenges. On the second day of the flight, Fowler virtually destroyed his machine in a crash near the town of Colfax, California. For the next four months, Fowler would

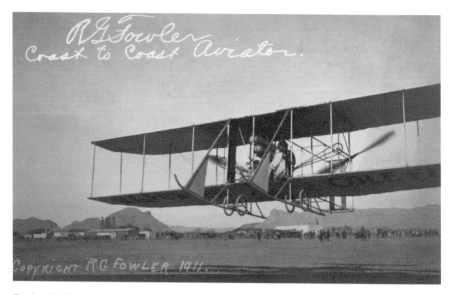

During his five-month transcontinental journey, Robert Fowler spent three weeks in Alabama, with much of that time devoted to making repairs to his flying machine.

overcome accidents, mechanical failures, inclement weather and other obstacles as he continued his eastward trek.

At one o'clock on the afternoon of January 10, 1912, almost four months after departing San Francisco, Robert Fowler maneuvered his flying machine to a landing in Mobile, Alabama. Remaining on the ground for only a few hours for a brief lunch and to refuel his machine, he departed for Flomaton, Alabama, following the tracks of the Louisville and Nashville Railroad. To create additional publicity for the flight, Fowler's manager, Charles Young, arranged a race between the passenger train and the aviator's flying machine. After giving the train a one-hour head start, Fowler would attempt to overtake it along the route. In an article describing the event, the Associated Press reported that Fowler and his flying machine landed a few minutes before five o'clock in the afternoon, ten minutes ahead of the train. By the end of the day, Fowler and his machine had traveled a remarkable 121 miles from Biloxi, Mississippi, by way of Mobile.

After spending the night in Flomaton, Fowler departed the following morning for Dothan, with planned stops in Evergreen, Georgiana and Andalusia to refuel his aircraft. After departing Evergreen, Fowler flew to Chapman and circled the big timber mill before proceeding on course along the Louisville and Nashville rail line to Georgiana. After he refueled and serviced his aircraft, Fowler continued to Andalusia, where he planned to provide a brief aerial demonstration for residents. According to the *Troy Messenger* newspaper, Fowler would then follow the rails of the Central Railroad of Georgia to Troy while traveling 3,500 feet in the air. The article advised readers that upon arrival in Troy, the aviator would circle the city once or twice and then alight at the fairgrounds. After taking time to rest and replenish his machine with gasoline and oil, Fowler would conduct an exhibition flight.

As had often been the case from the beginning of the transcontinental attempt, the flight would not be completed as planned. During the attempt takeoff at Georgiana, a propeller blade struck the soft ground and was destroyed. After completing the necessary repairs, Fowler continued to Andalusia, covering the thirty-one miles in twenty-nine minutes. During the next landing at Dozier, the aircraft again became stuck in the mud. Several hours were required to construct a short runway of wooden planks to provide a firm surface for takeoff. After fifteen minutes of flight, the aviator arrived over the rural community of Brantley for a brief stop to refuel his machine. On the subsequent takeoff, a gust of wind blew the machine off course. The landing gear of the machine collided with a stump, crushing one of the wheels and a propeller. Two weeks of labor and $1,000 in replacement parts shipped by rail from the Wright factory in Ohio would be required before the flight could be resumed.

In Troy, anxious residents awaited the arrival of the aviator. The editor of the *Troy Messenger* reported that the newspaper received 5,972 inquiries regarding the progress of repairs being made to the machine and the expected arrival of the aviator in the city. After receiving numerous requests for updates, a frustrated John Fowler advised reporters to no longer advertise an expected time of arrival but rather to look for him when they saw him.

On February 5, 1912, Fowler was finally able to resume his journey. In Troy, weather observer F.L. Zimmerman, keeper of the county clock, agreed to maintain surveillance from the clock tower, having his telescope in constant use to watch for the first appearance of the aviator. After performing a brief exhibition flight for residents of Troy, Fowler set a course over the tracks of the Atlantic Coast Line railroad to Dothan, his final landing site in the state of Alabama.

On February 8, 1912, John Fowler finally landed in Jacksonville, Florida. Arriving over the Moncrief Park Race Track at 4:30 p.m., Fowler circled the field three times and executed several dips and spiral dives over the crowd before bringing his machine down for a perfect landing. On February 17, 1912, after completing necessary repairs, Fowler departed Jacksonville and flew the remaining fifteen miles to land on the sands of Pablo Beach, the final segment of his five-month journey across the United States, an epic flight that included sixty-five forced landings. Upon his arrival, Fowler became the second aviator to complete the transcontinental challenge behind his rival, Calbraith Rodgers, who had suffered similar setbacks on his journey. By the time Rodgers arrived in California, his machine had been repaired so frequently that few pieces of the original craft remained. The prize money offered by William Randolph Hearst was not awarded because neither aviator completed his flight within the required thirty-day period.

The five-month transcontinental flight of Robert Fowler remains an obscure achievement in the history of aviation. Fowler attained success because of his sense of dedication and perseverance. During his journey across the nation, Fowler spent more than three weeks in Alabama, much of that time devoted to making repairs to his flying machine. However, the flight of Robert Fowler generated considerable enthusiasm for aviation among the residents of south Alabama. In time, the region would become the home of the Airbus United States Manufacturing Facility, the Coast Guard Aviation Training Center, Alabama Aviation College and Fort Novosel, the U.S. Army Aviation Training Center. The level of devotion and enthusiasm demonstrated by residents of south Alabama will ensure that the legacy of aviation in the region will continue to be preserved in the future.

THE STEAMSHIP AIRLINE

In the years following the Second World War, the management of several major American steamship companies took the unprecedented step of establishing airline operations as a means of supplementing their existing passenger transportation services. One of these companies, the Waterman Steamship Corporation of Mobile, would become the first airline to be established within the state of Alabama. Although the history of Waterman Airlines proved to be brief, its story was written in such diverse places as the capitals of Europe, jungle airstrips in South America and, ultimately, the U.S. Supreme Court.

The Civil Aeronautics Board, the agency established in 1938 to regulate aviation services in the United States, was responsible for issuing Certificates of Public Convenience and Necessity to allow private firms that were fit, willing and able to provide essential public transportation services. To qualify for a Certificate of Public Convenience and Necessity, the Waterman Steamship Corporation needed to establish non-scheduled airline service to demonstrate competency in providing scheduled air transportation services to the traveling public.

By 1939, the plan to provide aerial service to complement Waterman's well-established steamer service to Puerto Rico had been evaluated by company managers. In 1940, Waterman Steamship Corporation purchased a Lockheed Electra twin-engine aircraft to conduct survey flights on the proposed route. While the entry of the United States into the Second World War delayed inauguration of the airline service, Waterman management continued to develop the concept as war raged throughout Europe and Asia.

Carroll Barnett Waterman, son of the founder of the Waterman Steamship Corporation, became the driving force behind the creation of Waterman Airlines. A naval aviator during the Second World War, Carroll Waterman was assigned to the Naval Air Transport Service in the Pacific Theater in command of a Douglas R5D Skymaster four-engine transport aircraft, the navy version of the DC-4 civilian airliner. As an aircraft commander, Waterman was responsible for transporting troops and cargo between Oakland, California, and the embattled islands of the Pacific.

Immediately after the end of the war, Waterman returned to his role as vice-president of the Waterman Steamship Corporation and began finalizing plans to make his aerial luxury line a reality. The company soon completed the purchase five of Lockheed Lodestar twin-engine aircraft that had previously been utilized as navigation trainers for the military and placed in long-term storage in Augusta, Georgia, awaiting disposal. After concluding the transaction with the U.S. government, the aircraft were delivered to an overhaul and repair facility in Dallas, Texas, to be converted into civilian airline configurations. Waterman planned to utilize these aircraft to inaugurate the first intrastate airline service in the state of Alabama. To provide support for the new service, the company opened ticket offices in six cities: Mobile, Dothan, Montgomery, Birmingham, Huntsville and Muscle Shoals.

To operate the new airline, Carroll Waterman recruited former aviators of the Naval Air Transport Service and selected veterans of the Army Air Forces. Pilots serving as captains earned $600 per month, approximately $10,000 in 2023, while copilots received half of the pay of a captain. At the peak of operations, twenty-four pilots were employed by Waterman Airlines.

To attend to the needs of the passengers in flight, Carroll Waterman employed a small group of young women to serve as inflight hostesses. The position required applicants to be unmarried and a college graduate or registered nurse. The training program was straightforward: a trip to the airport to fly on one of the Waterman aircraft. Once airborne, the flight crew would provide instructions pertaining to passenger comfort, service and safety procedures. Fourteen cabin hostesses were employed to staff the fleet of aircraft.

On November 10, 1945, Chief Pilot J.W. Thornburg, assisted by Carroll Waterman, piloted the inaugural flight of Waterman Airlines. Because refurbishing of the Lockheed Lodestar aircraft had not yet been completed, passenger seats had not been installed. Instead, the aircraft was filled with boxes of flowers and a cargo of live lobsters in ice-filled garbage cans secured to the interior walls of the cabin to be delivered to elected officials in Birmingham for promotional purposes.

During the first months of operation, every flight proved to be an adventure. A typical workday involved fifteen hours on duty, with seven stops along the intrastate route. The flight crews learned to endure primitive conditions in the unpressurized, non-air-conditioned and noisy cabins of the Lockheed Lodestar, an aircraft having the reputation among Waterman pilots of being demanding and unforgiving to fly. Because airborne weather avoidance equipment was not readily available and the rudimentary navigation system of limited use, flight crews were essentially on their own once the flight was airborne en route to its next destination.

The operations center for Waterman Airlines was housed in a former military hangar at Bates Field. Constructed with funds provided by the War Assets Administration during the Second World War for use by the 18th Army Air Forces Glider Training Detachment, the building included areas designated for engine, radio and sheet metal repair with an inventory of spare parts to support a fleet of fifteen aircraft. The facility was staffed daily by three shifts of support personnel.

In addition to being a maintenance facility, the company utilized the hangar to train its flight crews. In addition to classroom instruction, the company purchased a Link trainer for pilots to maintain proficiency in maneuvering the aircraft by reference to flight instruments. Following an initial inspection of the training and maintenance facility, an inspector of the Civil Aeronautics Board determined that the airline exceeded federal standards governing operation of air carriers.

The fleet of surplus military aircraft used to inaugurate intrastate airline service proved to be a constant source of mechanical problems because of their extensive utilization during war. Even though former military technicians performed maintenance on the aircraft, they faced an almost impossible task in keeping the fleet operational. One of the most persistent problems was related to the design of the fuel system of the Lockheed Loadstar. In lieu of separate internal self-contained fuel tanks, designers used a wet wing concept in which the internal structure of the wing itself provided for the storage of fuel. Leaks became a constant source of mechanical delays and cancelations and, in one case, resulted in the loss of an aircraft that was destroyed on the ramp in Mobile when a fuel leak was ignited by an unknown source.

In August 1946, to improve schedule reliability, management of Waterman Airlines acquired three Douglas DC-3 aircraft. Originally produced as the military version C-47, the aircraft were retrofitted for civilian use by the Douglas Aircraft Company. The DC-3 first entered airline service in 1936 at American Airlines and would revolutionize air travel because of its speed and passenger comfort. Waterman utilized two of the aircraft on its intrastate routes and dedicated the third to non-scheduled passenger service between New York; Tampa, Florida; and San Juan, Puerto Rico.

Waterman
Air Cruises

**New York - New Orleans
to Puerto Rico
West Indies - Latin America**

Waterman Airlines, the air arm of the Waterman Steamship Corporation, advertised Air Cruise flights from New York to Puerto Rico and other international destinations.

In one example of the level of cooperation among the steamship and airline components of the company, a DC-3 flight crew landed in San Juan, Puerto Rico, during a labor strike and were unable to locate hotel accommodations. Upon learning that a Waterman steamship was in port at the company terminal across the harbor, the crew members made their way to the vessel and found accommodation in the comfortable passenger suites onboard.

In June 1946, Waterman Airlines obtained its first Douglas DC-4, a four-engine, long-range aircraft to be utilized on extended international flights. Because many of the Waterman pilots had flown the military version of the DC-4 during the war, the aircraft could be placed into service on an expedited schedule. The aircraft were modified with additional fuel tanks, allowing the DC-4 to remain airborne for about eighteen hours. A supplemental fifty-gallon oil tank, installed in the nose of the aircraft, allowed the engines to be serviced in-flight. To demonstrate the ability of Waterman Airlines to conduct international passenger operations, the DC-4 aircraft was utilized on flights to international destinations of Frankfurt, Germany; Johannesburg, South Africa; Hawaii; and Saudi Arabia.

Publicity brochures advertised flights on Waterman Airlines as "Air Cruises," non-scheduled flights for business and pleasure travel. In December 1946, staffed by a flight crew of nine, a Waterman Airlines DC-4 departed Mobile for an Air Cruise flight to Johannesburg, South Africa. After an initial stop in New York to board passengers, the flight traversed eighteen thousand miles during a ten-day period. Individual segments of the flight exceeded fifteen hours of flight time.

As personnel of Waterman Airlines continued to demonstrate proficiency in operating intrastate and international non-scheduled service, Juan Terry Trippe, the politically connected founder of Pan American Airways, petitioned the Civil Aeronautics Board to declare steamship airlines ineligible for the issuance of Certificates of Convenience and Necessity, even

Waterman became one of the first steamship companies to attempt to supplement its shipping service with air transportation. *John L. Marty Jr.*

though their operations were being conducted in accordance with federal requirements. Because the management of Pan American Airways had been helpful to the administration of President Franklin Roosevelt during the years of the Second World War, Trippe had powerful allies in Washington. To have Pan American designated as the international carrier of the United States, Juan Trippe used his political connections to eliminate competition that might infringe on that designation. In February 1947, the management of Waterman Airlines finally surrendered to the political pressure and ceased operations. In the spring of 1948, attorneys for Waterman Airlines filed an appeal to the U.S. Supreme Court. In a five-to-four decision, the court denied the application of Waterman Airlines to obtain a Certificate of Convenience and Necessity, an action that permanently grounded Alabama's airline.

The legacy of Waterman Airlines is that of an innovative concept that could not be fully developed because of the politics and protectionism that existed within the industry prior to the passage of the 1978 Airline Deregulation Act. Today, the concept of the Air Cruise is being developed by companies offering luxurious flights to exotic destinations around the world. For Waterman Airlines, however, it was a concept ahead of its time.

The Golden Age

The Golden Age of Aviation represents an era of significant aviation achievements and a period in which Alabama aviators earned international acclaim for their daring aerial exploits.

Alabama's First Ladies of Flight

Noted aviator Elinor Smith wrote, "To some young women with dreams of a wider world, there seems to be two paths to follow, each with great romantic appeal. One leads to Hollywood, the other to a career in the sky." During the early twentieth century, achieving success in the male-dominated aviation industry proved to be especially challenging for women. Rigid social attitudes branded aviation as not only inappropriate but also impractical because of the common belief that women lacked the physical strength to operate a flying machine. For two young women from Alabama, Katherine Stinson and Ruth Elder, the romantic appeal of a career in the sky not only created a path to a wider world but also established their equality as aviators while achieving international acclaim for their daring exploits and earning their rightful place in aviation history.

The eldest of four children, Katherine Stinson was born on Valentine's Day in 1891 in the rural community of Fort Payne, Alabama. Displaying a talent for music from an early age, Katherine dreamed of becoming a concert pianist. During her teenage years, she continued to develop her ability through music classes, private tutors and a year spent at a music conservatory. However, a trip to Kansas City in August 1911 significantly altered her future plans.

During her stay in Kansas City, the twenty-year-old Stinson learned that aeronaut Harry Eugene Honeywell would be conducting exhibition flights over the city in a hot-air balloon. To demonstrate the safety and reliability of lighter-than-air flight, Honeywell advertised his plan to take four female passengers aloft. The women would be randomly selected from a list of volunteers. Whether through divine intervention or sheer luck, Stinson was selected to make the flight. Once aloft, Stinson was amazed at the freedom she felt as she peered over the edge of the gondola at the city below. Her fascination with flight was further stimulated the next year as she accompanied a local aviator who was selling rides in an airplane near Hot Springs, Arkansas. The freedom she felt in the air combined with her keen sense of adventure convinced Stinson to abandon her musical prospects to pursue a future in the sky.

Initially, Stinson faced a seemingly insurmountable problem: finding a mentor willing to teach her to operate a flying machine. In 1912, less than a decade after the Wright brothers first achieved success in mechanical flight, fewer than two hundred licensed aviators existed in the world. Of these, only three were women. Visiting flying schools in St. Louis and other locations in the Midwest, Stinson was repeatedly advised to pursue a more suitable profession. Refusing to give up, she traveled to Cicero Field in Chicago in May 1912, where she met Maximilian Theodore Liljestrand, a Swedish immigrant who had recently organized a flying school. Even though Liljestrand, locally known as Max Lillie, initially refused to accept her as a student because of the common belief that women lacked the physical strength to manage a flying machine, Stinson used her powers of persuasion, and $250 in cash, to convince him to set aside his bias.

Confident and self-assured, Stinson proved an apt pupil. In July 1912, after only four hours and ten minutes of instruction, she operated the Wright Model B airplane in flight without the assistance of her instructor. Three days later, Stinson performed a figure-eight maneuver and made an ascent to an altitude of five hundred feet to complete the requirements for a license issued by the Federation Aeronautique Internationale, the international entity formed to advance the science and sport of aeronautics prior to the establishment of a similar governing body in the United States. In achieving this milestone, Katherine Stinson became the fourth female aviator in the United States to earn a license to operate a flying machine.

Katherine Stinson of Fort Payne, Alabama, became the fourth female aviator in the United States to earn a license to operate a flying machine. *UNM Libraries.*

In April 1913, Katherine and her mother invested approximately $10,000 to form the Stinson Aviation Company, a firm established to manufacture, sell, rent and otherwise engage in the trade of aircraft. The company's first asset was a Wright Model B airplane obtained from Max Lillie to enable Stinson to earn money demonstrating her skills as an exhibition pilot at aviation meets, county fairs and other public gatherings.

By the summer of 1913, Stinson's career as an exhibition pilot had literally taken off, with appearances throughout the Midwest. With her long black hair cascading down her back, the curls adorned with colorful ribbons, Katherine Stinson charmed crowds wherever she performed. A reporter for a Kansas City newspaper described the five-foot, one-hundred-pound aviator as a young woman who looked like a sophomore in high school. Because of her youthful appearance, event organizers began to promote her as the "Flying Schoolgirl."

As an exhibition pilot, Stinson became the first woman to perform several difficult and dangerous maneuvers. In July 1915, she became the first woman to perform an aerial loop in an airplane while performing over Cecil Field in Chicago. However, most of Stinson's pioneering flights were made to advance aviation. In September 1913, she became the first woman to be authorized by the U.S. Postal Service to transport mail by airplane during an appearance at the state fair in Helena, Montana. Stinson flew from a temporary facility on the fairgrounds, making daily flights to the Helena Post Office. During the four-day exhibition, she delivered more than one thousand letters and postcards. In November 1914, Stinson became the first aviator in Alabama to deliver mail by airplane when the postmaster of Troy authorized aerial service from the Pike County Fair. Departing from the fairgrounds, Stinson circled her machine over the post office, where she dropped a bag of mail to a postal employee stationed on the ground below.

In December 1916, Stinson earned a reputation as a world-renowned aviator when she sailed for Asia to fulfill a six-month contract to perform in Japan and China. Initially appearing before twenty-five thousand spectators during a night aerial exhibition at the Aoyama Parade Grounds in Tokyo, she became the first woman to perform in the skies over Japan. As a female aviator, her presence in a society that restricted women to subservient roles created great enthusiasm throughout Japan. Stinson later wrote, "The women have simply overwhelmed me with attention and seem to regard me as their emancipator."

Leaving Japan, Stinson performed in Peking, China, during a private premiere for President Li Yung Hung at the Sacred Temple of Agriculture. The Chinese president was so impressed by her performance that he bestowed on her the title "Granddaughter of Heaven." Her aerial tour of China included demonstration flights in Canton, Hong Kong, Tientsin, Nanking and Shanghai. In April 1917, Stinson's Asian tour ended two months early, as the United States Congress adopted a resolution of war against the Imperial German government, elevating the conflict in Europe into the First World War.

Returning to America, Stinson immediately began to lobby officials of the Armed Forces to allow her to participate in the war effort by volunteering for the Air Service, the aviation section of the U.S. Army. Their response was polite but firm: women would not be accepted for combat service. Undaunted, she sought other opportunities to do her part. She volunteered to solicit contributions for the American Red Cross by making a publicity flight from Buffalo, New York, to Washington, D.C., with appearances in New York City and Philadelphia. Departing on June 24, 1917, she bombarded towns along the route with pamphlets urging citizens to contribute to the Red Cross. The airplane used for the flight, a Curtiss "Jenny" military trainer, was equipped with a small mirror in the cockpit to allow Stinson to

During her career, Katherine Stinson set multiple aviation records and became a world-renowned aviator. *UNM Libraries*.

present a clean face, free of oil discharged from the engine, before greeting crowds at each stop.

At the completion of her flight, Stinson circled the Washington Monument before performing a series of aerial maneuvers for the crowd of five thousand spectators who gathered to celebrate her arrival. After landing at the nearby polo grounds, she was escorted to the front steps of the Capitol building to deliver $2 million in pledges to Secretary of the Treasury William McAdoo.

Unable to persuade military officials to allow her to apply her aviation skills to the war effort, Stinson continued to demonstrate her aeronautical abilities in the United States. On the morning of December 11, 1917, Stinson departed the airfield at North Island near San Diego, California. Landing in San Francisco after a nonstop flight of 610 miles and nine hours and ten minutes aloft, she established a national record for distance and duration.

Even though she continued to maintain an active flying schedule, Stinson continued her efforts to participate in the war. Eventually, she volunteered as a driver for an ambulance service organized under the American Red Cross. Her tour of duty in France was brief because of the November 1918 Armistice that brought an end to the hostilities. Stinson soon learned that she would be authorized to transport mail by air for the American military along a route between Germany and France. Before beginning the flights, however, Stinson contracted what was thought to be a serious cold. Her illness was soon diagnosed as tuberculosis, a disease that would do what early twentieth-century societal standards and a male-dominated aviation industry could not: bring an end to the aviation career of the Flying Schoolgirl. Stinson spent the remainder of her life working as a prominent architect from an office in Santa Fe, New Mexico. Because of recurring effects of tuberculosis, Katherine Stinson would never again pilot an airplane. The notable life of Katherine Stinson came to an end on July 8, 1977, at her home in Santa Fe. She was posthumously inducted into the National Aviation Hall of Fame, the International Aviation and Space Hall of Fame in San Diego, California, and the Alabama Aviation Hall of Fame in Birmingham.

Although the accomplishments of Katherine Stinson shattered many of the stereotypes that precluded women from participating in aviation, opportunities for women remained elusive. For Alabama native Ruth Elder, the dream of a wider world that would lead to Hollywood began with a path through the sky.

Born in Anniston, Alabama, on September 8, 1902, Ruth Elder and her family lived in a modest home on Noble Street. Friends of the family described Ruth as a flamboyant and extroverted child who seemed destined for things greater than the small community of Anniston could provide. Following graduation from high school, the eighteen-year-old left her home in Anniston seeking the excitement of the city. After relocating to Birmingham, Elder found employment as a clerk in a department store. Elder soon wed Anniston schoolteacher Claude Moody in what would be the first of six marriages to five husbands. Filing for divorce after only two years, Elder soon wed Lyle Womack, a self-described entrepreneur from Pennsylvania. The newlyweds left Birmingham for Lakeland, Florida, where Ruth obtained employment as a receptionist in a dental office. Elder quickly realized that a domestic life did not suit her adventurous personality, and she began to have second thoughts about her future.

The years following the end of the First World War began the era that would become known as the Golden Age of Aviation, a time during which an aviator who achieved a noteworthy milestone such as setting a speed, distance, altitude or endurance record became an overnight celebrity glorified by the media. The excitement and sense of adventure associated with aviation immediately appealed to Elder. Swept up in the romance and glamour of aviators and their exploits, Elder visited the local airport and attempted to convince flying instructor George Haldeman to teach her to operate an aircraft. Haldeman immediately rejected the idea because he believed women to be unsuitable as aviators because of their fragile emotions. After enduring weeks of persuasion, Haldeman relented and accepted Elder as a student. During the next two years, Elder continued her training as money permitted, although she could not afford the luxury of flying as frequently as she desired.

In May 1927, a twenty-five-year-old airmail pilot named Charles Lindbergh astounded the world by completing a nonstop flight across the Atlantic Ocean from New York to Paris. The thirty-three-hour flight served as a catalyst for an emerging aviation industry and would significantly impact the life of Ruth Elder. Before Lindbergh returned to a hero's welcome in New York, Elder made the decision to become the first woman to cross the Atlantic Ocean by airplane.

In the weeks following her decision to replicate the epic flight of Charles Lindbergh, Elder received unexpected support. A group of West Virginia business owners, recognizing an opportunity to take advantage of the publicity surrounding the Lindbergh flight, decided to provide financial support for an attempt by a female aviator to be the first to cross the Atlantic Ocean by airplane. The investors faced two critical decisions that would determine the success of their plan: purchasing an airplane capable of making the flight and the selection of the perfect female aviator to capture the hearts and attention of an air-minded public.

Elder provided the perfect face for the venture. Allen Churchill, a reporter for the *New York Times*, wrote, "With her wide smile, she looked exactly like the Pepsodent advertisements in contemporary magazines." An article in the Defiance, Ohio *Crescent News* described Elder as the fairest of the brave and the bravest of the fair. Asked why she would attempt such a dangerous flight, Elder replied, "I've lived for a while without amounting to a plugged nickel. I want to do something that will make people notice me, that may give me an opportunity to get somewhere in the world." Because of her limited experience, Elder recruited her instructor George Haldeman to accompany her on the flight. Ironically, the investment group financing the project selected a Stinson Detroiter aircraft for the transatlantic attempt, a design created by Eddie Stinson, brother of Katherine Stinson.

In September 1927, only two years after making her first flight in an airplane, Elder arrived at Roosevelt Field on Long Island, New York, to begin preparations for her highly publicized flight. Newspapers reported that Ruth Elder breezed into Long Island with the subtlety of a gale. Her

Ruth Elder of Anniston earned the titles of "Miss America of Aviation" and the "Flying Flapper."

brown hair was bobbed in the latest style, and the Alabama native almost never appeared without a rainbow-hued scarf wrapped around her head, pinning back her wild curls.

Her airplane, christened the *American Girl*, was equally bold, painted in a brilliant shade of orange. The color had less to do with the flair of its pilot than practicality. In the wide expanse of the deep blue-gray waters of the Atlantic Ocean, the floating wreckage of an orange airplane would be more visible to searchers. In recognition of her West Virginia financial supporters, "Wheeling, USA" was painted on the exterior fuselage.

Even considering Lindbergh's successful flight, attempting to navigate across the Atlantic Ocean by airplane in 1927 was an extremely dangerous endeavor. In August of that year, sixteen people died attempting oceanic flights. Because of the increasing number of fatalities, officials in the United States and Canada pressured lawmakers to ban or strictly regulate oceanic flights. Experiencing weeks of bureaucratic delays awaiting approval for the flight, Elder refused to give up. She endured the constant attention of reporters and critics, submitted to every test required by local officials, qualified for a pilot's license, completed a physical examination and demonstrated her proficiency as a pilot in the *American Girl* in the presence of the assembled crowds. Finally, on October 11, 1927, Ruth Elder and George Haldeman received official clearance for their flight from New York to Paris.

On the morning of departure, Elder boarded the aircraft with a basket of food on her arm, appearing as though she was on her way to a picnic. Inside the basket, she carried basic rations for the trip: twelve sandwiches, six bars of chocolate, four dill pickles, two quarts of coffee and one quart of beef tea. Elder was outfitted in tan knickers, a green and red plaid sweater with matching golf stockings and her trademark rainbow-colored ribbon around her head, an accessory known in New York fashion circles as a Ruth Ribbon. Her pocket held a complete vanity case with lipstick, rouge and other cosmetics. Elder explained, "I want to get out of the airplane in Paris as cool and neat as I did at the start. I'll powder my nose whenever I feel like it, flying or not flying." Two rubber suits reported to be capable of keeping Elder and Haldeman afloat for up to seventy-two hours in the frigid Atlantic Ocean were also stored in the aircraft should an emergency landing become necessary.

Just before five o'clock on the evening of October 11, 1927, the *American Girl* lifted off from the same Roosevelt Field runway used by Charles Lindbergh. The assembled crowd of more than five hundred spectators cheered wildly as the huge aircraft lifted off with only six hundred feet of runway remaining.

Throughout the first night of the flight, Elder and Haldeman took turns at the controls of the aircraft, singing songs to pass the time as the *American Girl* traversed the darkness. The next morning, after fifteen hours aloft but having traveled less than half of the distance to their destination, the flight began to encounter difficulties. The airplane had been flying into a steady headwind since leaving New York, causing fuel consumption to increase significantly. More troubling, the *American Girl* had begun to leak lubricating oil, the lifeblood of the engine.

By the second morning, thirty-two hours after takeoff but still eight hours from landfall on the coast of England, Elder and Haldeman were faced with a life-threatening decision: continue to fly until the loss of oil caused a failure of the engine or attempt an immediate landing on the surface of the ocean in the hope of being rescued by a passing ship. As they prepared for the worst, they spotted a Dutch oil tanker, the *Barendrecht*, that appeared like a miracle on the surface of the ocean. It was the first ship they had observed in more than twelve hours.

In October 1927, Ruth Elder became the first woman to attempt a nonstop flight across the Atlantic Ocean by airplane. *Roger Q. Williams Papers.*

After dropping a note onto the deck of the ship to advise the crew of their intentions, Elder and Haldeman steered their aircraft to a touchdown on the surface of the ocean. Wet and fatigued, they were quickly hoisted onboard the Dutch tanker. Shortly after Elder and Haldeman abandoned their aircraft, the *American Girl* burst into flames and began to slip slowly into the sea, sinking to a watery grave in the depths of the Atlantic Ocean.

Elder's attempt to be the first woman to cross the Atlantic Ocean has been termed a glorious failure. Although the flight did not reach its destination, it did represent an overwater endurance record of 2,623 miles, the longest flight ever made by a woman. Arriving in Europe by ship instead of airplane, Elder was nevertheless feted by an adoring public. For publicity purposes, United Press International leased an airplane to allow Elder to make a landing at the Le Bourget airdrome in Paris, her flight's intended destination.

Upon her return to New York City, her ship was met by adoring crowds, news reporters and a ticker-tape parade. Two days later, she attended a Washington luncheon hosted by President Calvin Coolidge, joining Charles Lindbergh, Richard E. Byrd, Amelia Earhart and other distinguished aviators. Most enticing for Elder were the numerous offers that arrived from Hollywood, offering as much as $400,000 for her story, a sum equivalent to more than $6 million in 2023 dollars. For twenty-five-year-old Elder, the dream of a wider world that began on Noble Street in Anniston would now lead to the romantic appeal of Hollywood.

Labeled by reporters as "Miss America of Aviation" and the "Florida Flying Flapper," Elder quickly capitalized on her notoriety by signing a contract for a twenty-five-week tour of vaudeville shows and other appearances at the weekly rate of $5,000. After six months of stage performances, she moved to Hollywood to star in two silent movies, *Moran of the Marines* and *The Winged Horseman*. Although acting, hosting luncheons and attending parties occupied most of her days, Elder did take time to continue to sharpen her flying skills.

In August 1929, Elder joined nineteen other female aviators in the first Women's Air Derby from Santa Monica, California, to Cleveland, Ohio, a contest humorist Will Rogers referred to as the Powder Puff Derby. Overcoming a mechanical failure that resulted in an emergency landing, Elder finished fifth of fourteen aircraft that completed the 2,759-mile race. Amelia Earhart, who became the first woman to successfully navigate the Atlantic Ocean by air in June 1928, finished only two places ahead of Elder.

Two months later, Elder assisted in organizing the first association of female aviators. Because 99 of the 117 licensed female pilots in the

United States initially agreed to join the organization, the group became known as the Ninety-Nines. Today, the membership consists of more than 150 chapters worldwide. Elder would continue her membership in the organization until her death.

Flying an airplane was the one aspect of her life that Ruth Elder seemed able to control. In later years, she would confess that the money she had earned slipped through her fingers, and soon there was nothing. In 1955, the reclusive billionaire and owner of Hughes Aircraft, Howard Hughes, became aware of Elder's financial difficulties. Having an affinity for individuals who had achieved notable firsts in aviation, Hughes convinced Elder to accept a position as a secretary at Hughes Aircraft. In a sense, her life had come full circle, beginning as an unknown stenographer from a small Alabama town and ending up as an unrecognized secretary in a large aerospace firm.

Elder would never reclaim the flamboyant and exciting lifestyle that she so desperately sought early in her life. On October 9, 1977, just two days before the fiftieth anniversary of her historic flight, Ruth Elder died peacefully at her home in California. Fittingly, her ashes were scattered from the cockpit of an airplane over the Pacific Ocean.

Amelia Earhart once wrote, "Some of us have great runways already built for us. If you have one, take off. But if you don't have one, realize it is your responsibility to grab a shovel and build one for yourself and for those who follow." Katherine Stinson and Ruth Elder, Alabama's first ladies of flight, not only built runways to fulfill their dreams but also used those runways to create opportunity and equality in the sky for future generations of women who shared their self-reliance, sense of adventure and love of flight.

SKEETS ELLIOTT, THE ALABAMA EAGLE

In November 1916, President Woodrow Wilson was reelected to a second term on the platform that he kept the nation out of the war that raged in Europe. By the time he took the oath of office in March 1917, the situation had changed dramatically. Ongoing attacks by German submarines on civilian ships operating under the flag of the United States convinced Wilson that the nation could no longer maintain its neutrality. In April 1917, he formally requested that Congress adopt a declaration of war against the Imperial German government, an action that elevated the conflict into the First World War.

Woefully unprepared for armed intervention in Europe, the federal government immediately initiated a massive expansion of its military forces. Unlike previous conflicts, the development of the airplane as a tactical weapon would significantly affect military planning and strategy. In July 1917, faced with an immediate need for aircraft and pilots, Congress appropriated $640 million, the largest sum ever authorized for a single purpose, the production of aircraft and construction of training fields needed to produce six thousand military aviators for service overseas.

Like many young men of the period, Milton Elliott was attracted to the romance and adventure of aviation. Born on April 24, 1891, into one of the most influential families in Gadsden, Alabama, Elliot's father founded Elliott Car Works, a manufacturer of streetcars used for public transportation. The Elliott home was an enormous Victorian-style structure that stood on the site of the present-day Etowah County Courthouse. Described as a lanky, ordinary-looking young man, Milton Elliott first attended Columbia University in New York City before becoming a member of the Sigma Alpha Epsilon fraternity at the University of Alabama. Even though his application for military service had previously been denied for being underweight, Elliott was accepted as a cadet of the Army Air Service during the summer of 1917 and assigned to flight training at Barron Field near Fort Worth, Texas.

Known as "Skeets" by fellow cadets, Elliott proved to be an exceptional student and soon earned a commission as a second lieutenant. While stationed at Barron Field, Elliott developed a close friendship with another cadet, Ormer Locklear. A native of Texas, Locklear quickly earned a reputation as a daredevil pilot who was always one step ahead of a court-martial. On one early training flight in a Curtiss JN-4 "Jenny" aircraft, Locklear noticed that the cap on the aircraft's radiator had become loose, allowing water to escape overboard. Realizing that the engine would soon fail because of overheating, Locklear climbed from the front pilot position of the tandem seat aircraft onto the wing while his flight instructor controlled the machine from the rear seat. Grasping the wing strut to brace against the slipstream of the propeller, Locklear replaced the loose radiator cap, preventing an emergency landing. The excitement and lure of the experience became too powerful for Ormer Locklear to ever return to the routine of basic flight training maneuvers.

Described as inseparable friends, Locklear and Skeets Elliott began practicing aerial stunts while maintaining a safe distance from Barron Field to prevent being disciplined for conducting unauthorized maneuvers. Eventually, a superior officer discovered the antics of Locklear and Elliott.

Instead of being reprimanded, the duo was assigned the tasks of performing their in-flight wing-walking skills to student aviators to instill confidence in handling the airplane and to demonstrate that midair rescues could be made from disabled aircraft. In November 1918, Locklear became the first to complete a transfer from one airplane to another while inflight. Skeets Elliott piloted one of the aircraft, while a mutual friend, James Frew, piloted the second machine.

After the war, Locklear and Elliott elected to remain in the military to enjoy the luxury of flying at government expense. In December 1918, Ormer Locklear became commanding officer of B Squadron at Barron Field, while Skeets Elliott was promoted to command C Squadron. During this period, Locklear, Elliott and new team addition, Lieutenant Shirley Short, worked to perfect the in-flight airplane-to-airplane transfer. This maneuver required the two Curtiss "Jenny" biplanes to fly in proximity so that the upper wing of Short's airplane would almost touch the lower wing of Elliot's machine. Positioned on the upper wing of Short's airplane, Locklear would grasp the curved wing-skid on the lower wing of the Elliott machine. After transferring to the second aircraft, he would make his way along the wing to the empty front pilot position.

Milton "Skeets" Elliott (*right*) of Gadsden with Ormer Locklear (*center*) and S.J. Short of the Locklear Flying Circus. *Library of Congress.*

Skeets Elliott pilots a Curtiss JN-4 "Jenny," with Ormer Locklear hanging from the landing gear while performing one of their death-defying aerial stunts. *University of Texas.*

Recognizing the opportunity for fame and fortune in the years following the First World War, the trio discharged from the military in May 1919 and entered a business arrangement with promoter William Hickman Pickens, a man described as the greatest publicity merchant ever to walk in shoe leather. Under Pickens's management, the Locklear Flying Circus received appearance fees of $3,000 per day, with considerably higher amounts earned for a full week of aerial exhibitions. Considering an average annual household income of $3,300 in 1919, Locklear, Skeets Elliott and Shirley Short were considered among the highest paid entertainers of the period.

In October 1919, the Locklear Flying Circus attracted the largest crowd to ever assemble in the state during an appearance at the Alabama State Fair. Proclaimed as the most awe-inspiring and bewildering feat to be witnessed through the nineteen centuries of civilization, the performance in Birmingham included the first public attempt by Locklear to transfer from an airplane flown by Skeets Elliot to a speeding car and back again. At the conclusion of their performance in Birmingham, Skeets Elliot returned to Gadsden for a few days to visit with his mother, who constantly worried about the activities of her son. Nina Elliot deplored her son's occupation, stating, "He does not have to fly for a living, but he is charmed by the life and its associations. I cannot induce him to remain at home. I know Milton will be killed someday. It is only a question of time, but I will try to reconcile myself to it."

In November 1919, the Locklear Flying Circus flew its last show before leaving for Hollywood and the allure of the silver screen. Having already performed aerial stunts for the feature film *The Great Air Robbery* earlier in the year, Locklear, Elliott and Short were scheduled to begin production of *The Skywayman* in June 1920, a film that would include aerial stunts more daring than ever recorded. During their time in Hollywood, the young aviators attended Thursday night dances at the Hollywood Hotel and were on a first-name basis with Mary Pickford, Buster Keaton and other celebrities.

Although the script of the film included two very hazardous stunts, crashing an airplane into a church steeple and the first airplane-to-train transfer, the most dangerous would be a low-altitude spinning maneuver performed at night. The maneuver required the airplane to be slowed to a speed insufficient for the wings to maintain enough lifting force to remain aloft. As the airplane began to descend, the pilot would manipulate the controls to force the wings to rotate in a spinning motion. Although the stunt was originally scheduled to be filmed during daylight hours with the cameras fitted with red filters to simulate darkness, Locklear demanded that the maneuver be performed at night to enhance his reputation as the "Daredevil of the Air."

Large studio arc lights were set up to illuminate the Curtiss "Jenny" aircraft throughout the spin maneuver. As the aircraft descended to about five hundred feet above the ground, the lights were to be turned off as a signal for the pilot to recover from the steep descent. Because recovery from the maneuver would be initiated from a very low altitude, the timing would be vital.

On the night of August 2, 1920, a large crowd gathered to witness filming of the stunt. During preflight inspection of the aircraft, Ormer Locklear confided to his close friend Skeets Elliott that he had a hunch that he shouldn't fly that evening. Elliott would jokingly respond that his friend was becoming an old timer and getting old maid ideas. For the first time, Elliott positioned himself in the front pilot station of the aircraft. In every other performance, he had occupied the rear seat.

Beginning the maneuver at an altitude of 2,000 feet above the ground, Elliott and Locklear began spiraling down while illuminated by the beams of the arc lights. As the plane reached the altitude designated for recovery, the lights remained illuminated, the operators failing to extinguish them as prearranged. The airplane continued to descend and plunged into the ground. Ormer Locklear and Skeets Elliott, the Alabama Eagle, were killed instantly. A watch worn by Elliott stopped at 10:09 p.m. Four silver dollars found in his pocket were melted together because of the intense heat from a fire that resulted from a ruptured fuel tank.

The *Los Angeles Times* newspaper reported that Hollywood had never seen a funeral like the one staged for Ormer Locklear and Skeets Elliott. It would not see a comparable one until six years later, when the silent film star Rudolph Valentino was laid to rest. As the flag-draped caskets of the inseparable companions in life and in death were transported to the train station, eighteen airplanes flown by noted Hollywood stunt pilots circled overhead, dropping thousands of rose petals on the two gray hearses. The funeral procession included the twenty-four-piece Los Angeles Police Department band and more than two hundred automobiles. Twenty mounted cowboys from Fox Studios adorned in ten-gallon hats and chaps accompanied the procession, while a Goodyear blimp floated silently overhead, maintaining pace with the hearses.

The body of Milton "Skeets" Elliott arrived at the Gadsden train depot at 10:00 a.m. on the morning of August 9, 1920, the day after his friend Ormer Locklear was buried in Fort Worth, Texas. An American Legion Honor Guard escorted the casket from the depot to his boyhood home, where a funeral service, attended by hundreds of Gadsden residents, was held on the veranda. After the service, the American Legion Honor Guard and former members of the United States military escorted the casket to Forest Cemetery. During the ceremony, the City of Gadsden suspended all operations, and downtown merchants closed their doors in respect for the fallen aviator. An article in the *Gadsden Evening Journal* reported that all attention was concentrated on the final tribute to the beloved Gadsden boy.

In September 1920, Fox Studios released *The Skywayman*, the feature film in which Locklear and Elliott lost their lives. The studio agreed to donate 10 percent of the profits from the movie to the families of the pilots. In Gadsden, the Belle Theater was the first in the South to premiere the film, which was advertised to include the thrilling and heart-stopping acts of Ormer Locklear and Milton Elliott and, notably, the final scene in which the aviators perished.

In a special press release, studio president William Fox wrote, "Not in challenging fate but in serving mankind, Lieuts. Ormer Locklear and Milton Elliott gave their lives. Together they rode the winds seeking new paths in the untracked skies. Explorers of the air charted the perilous clouds, where they led in danger others might follow in safety. They knew the odds and faced them gladly. They will be remembered as two American soldiers who counted their lives a little thing to give in a noble cause for the future good of country and mankind."

The aviation career of Milton Elliott was tragically short, lasting only three brief years. During that time, however, Elliott and Ormer Locklear became national celebrities because of their daring exploits in the air. As early pioneers and performers who introduced the airplane to people in cities and communities across country, Elliott and Locklear epitomized the glamour and romance of flying during the Golden Age of Aviation. The career and success of Ormer Locklear, known as the man who walked on wings, would have never been possible without his friend in life and companion in death, the Alabama Eagle, Milton "Skeets" Elliott.

THE GREAT BALLOON RACE

On a fall afternoon in October 1920, college football became the second-most popular team sport in Alabama as aeronauts from four countries assembled on the grounds of the North Alabama By-Products Coke Oven plant in Tarrant for the start of the Gordon Bennett Trophy International Balloon Race, the premier event of world balloon racing. Anticipating a massive turnout of spectators for the event, the Birmingham Police Department issued press releases requesting those attending the race to arrive at the balloon field early to prevent the road to Rickwood Field from being blocked as fans made their way home following the conclusion of the Auburn-Vanderbilt football game.

The 1920 International Balloon Race was the ninth in a series of races sponsored by James Gordon Bennett Jr., publisher of the *New York Herald* newspaper. According to organizers, the goal of the race was simple: to fly the greatest straight-line distance from the launch site. The winning team would earn the privilege of hosting the event in their home country the following year. The team that succeeded in winning three consecutive international races would be awarded permanent possession of the Gordon Bennett trophy.

In 1913, the American team of Ralph Upson and Ralph Preston, flying the balloon *Goodyear*, won the race that originated in Paris, France, by completing a flight of 618 kilometers (384 miles) in forty-eight hours, thirty minutes. Subsequent races were canceled because of the First World War in Europe.

Because the American team had been victorious in the last race held prior to the war, the United States would host the 1920 event, the first to be held since the cessation of hostilities in Europe. According to an article published in the *Birmingham News*, the enthusiasm and drive of the local American Legion Post made it possible for the city to host a National Elimination Balloon Race in September, followed by the international race in October.

The race was celebrated as the first international sports event to be held in the South, and organizers in Birmingham proclaimed that the city would unquestionably earn words of desirable publicity that would place the name of the city on the lips of thousands of persons all over the United States. The fame of Birmingham as the only city in the country able to offer ideal conditions for the start of such a race would be carried to the four corners of the earth.

The September elimination race was open only to citizens of the United States. Teams that achieved the three highest finishing positions would represent the United States in the international competition. The top three teams qualifying for the International Balloon Race included the *U.S. Army No. 1*, piloted by Lieutenant Thompson and Captain Weeks; *Kansas City II*, piloted by Henry E. Honeywell; and the *Goodyear II*, piloted by Ralph Upson, winner of the 1913 international competition.

The international event utilized the same facility used to launch the balloons in the elimination race, a large field adjacent to the North Birmingham By-Products Coke Oven plant. Founded in 1920 by the Sloss-Sheffield Steel and Iron Company, the plant produced metallurgical coke, a raw material used in blast furnaces in Birmingham to produce iron. Hydrogen, a by-product of the process, was supplied from large gas mains to inflate the balloons on the field.

The international race included seven balloons from four countries: the United States, Belgium, Italy and France. Teams from Germany and Austria were excluded from international sporting events because of sanctions imposed on those countries following the conclusion of the First World War. Although Labrador, a geographic region within the Canadian Province of Newfoundland, was designated the termination point of the race, the team that achieved the greatest distance along a path from Birmingham to Labrador would be declared the winner.

During the seven days prior to the race, designated by organizers as Balloon Week, the *Birmingham News* reported that colorful uniforms of

Competitors in the 1920 International Balloon Race utilized the grounds of the North Birmingham By-Products Coke Oven Plant.

Contestants and dignitaries gather before the start of the 1920 International Balloon Race in Birmingham.

foreign countries were prominent in the streets of the city. The French team was lauded on Wednesday before the race with a luncheon at the Tutwiler Hotel. The day concluded with a dinner and dance held later in the evening. Similar activities were hosted for visiting dignitaries from Belgium and Italy.

On Saturday, October 23, more than fifty thousand spectators assembled to enjoy a band concert and spectacular aerial demonstration by the pilots of two airplanes that performed death-defying stunts before the start of the International Balloon Race. At 4:15 p.m., the balloon *Birmingham* was launched to evaluate weather conditions. Piloted by Roy Donaldson, the balloon also carried representatives of the *Birmingham News*, the *Birmingham Age-Herald* and the chamber of commerce. The French army balloon *Lorraine* followed the *Birmingham*. The *U.S. Army No. 1*, the *Belgica* of Belgium, the *Kansas City II*, the *Aduens* and *Trumphale IV* of Italy and the *Goodyear II* were launched at intervals of five minutes until all balloons were aloft.

During the launch of the *Aduens* and the *Trumphale IV*, an Italian band performed a rousing rendition of the Italian anthem. Accompanied by the loud cheers of Birmingham's large Italian community, the pilot of the *Aduens*, Major Valle, who was dressed in full military regalia, thanked them with a brief speech in his native language as the balloon carried him overhead.

Competitors from seven countries participated in the 1920 International Balloon Race.

Once aloft, the seven balloons drifted slowly to the northeast, pushed by prevailing winds. Bathed in the soft glow of the setting sun, the airships displayed a majestic panorama of colors as they faded from sight.

The pilot balloon *Birmingham* landed in a cornfield one minute before noon the following day, as agreed on by race officials. The crew of the *Belgica* set down at North Hero Island in Lake Champlain (located on the border of Vermont and Canada) after remaining aloft for forty hours and fifteen minutes, having achieved the race-winning distance of 1,769 kilometers (1,100 miles). The *Kansas City II*, piloted by Harry Honeywell, set a United States endurance record by remaining aloft for forty-eight hours and twenty-six minutes but fell short of the distance attained by the *Belgica*. The Italian teams completed the race in third and fourth positions. The *Goodyear II* finished fifth, followed by the *U.S. Army No. 1* and the *Lorraine* of France, finishing in last place.

In winning the 1920 International Balloon Race, the crew of the *Belgica*, was honored at an Aero Club of America banquet held in New York City. In addition to securing Belgium the privilege of hosting the international race the next year, the crew received a $1,000 cash prize and the Civitan Club Mileage Trophy.

The success of the 1920 Elimination and International Balloon Races made Birmingham the logical choice to host the 1921 National Balloon Race. Selected as the host city by the Aero Club of America, the 1921 race became the main attraction of the city's Semi-Centennial Celebration. The winner of the race would represent the United States in the international competition to be held in Belgium.

To generate funding for the event, children could purchase up to five postcards of Birmingham or any other town in Alabama. The postcards would be stamped and self-addressed before being collected at a balloon post office on the launch site. Each postcard would be stamped with the name of the balloon slated to carry it aloft. According to an article in the *Birmingham News*, the cards would then be dropped from the balloon along the path of flight. A cash prize of ten dollars would be awarded to the child whose card was returned from the most distant city.

Nine balloons were launched on the evening of May 21, 1921, under the light of a brilliant moon from the same site used during the previous races. Winner of the 1913 International Balloon Race, Ralph Upson, served as the pilot of the *Birmingham Semi-Centennial* balloon, accompanied by C.G. Andrus of the United States Weather Bureau. After thirty-four hours and forty minutes aloft, Upson and Andrus set the *Birmingham Semi-Centennial* down in a field near Stuart, Virginia, achieving a race-winning distance of 423 miles. As the balloon descended for landing, a crowd of spectators gathered nearby to observe the unusual activity. One spectator in the crowd fainted because of a belief that the arrival of the balloon signified the end of the world.

The dominance of the lighter-than-air airships began to decline following the end of the First World War. Because surplus military aircraft could be purchased for a fraction of the cost of a balloon, landing fields for airplanes soon replaced landing sites for balloons. For a brief period in 1920, however, the name of Birmingham, host city of the International Balloon Race, was placed on the lips of thousands of persons all over the United States and carried to the four corners of the earth.

THE GADSDEN BLIMP HANGAR

On July 11, 1929, the front page of the *Birmingham News* included coverage of the dedication ceremony of the new Goodyear Tire and Rubber Company plant in Gadsden. The new manufacturing facility was described as the finest and most modern automobile tire plant in the entire country. A crowd of more than ten thousand guests attended the festivities, a ceremony highlighted by an electric signal sent by President Herbert Hoover from Washington, D.C., to raise the large American flag over the administration building, an act that officially opened the plant for production. Visitors were allowed to tour the massive buildings that would employ seven hundred of their fellow residents. However, one of the most remarkable structures on the grounds of the plant would not be utilized to produce automobile tires. It was designed to shelter the company's newest method of aerial advertising, the Goodyear blimp.

In addition to being known as the producer of quality tires for automobiles, the Goodyear Company was equally renowned for its use of blimps for publicity. In June 1925, Goodyear launched the blimp *Pilgrim*, the first in what would become its fleet of airships. *Pilgrim* was the first blimp to utilize helium gas rather than the more flammable hydrogen as its lifting agent. Goodyear dispatched *Pilgrim* to special events and large assemblies throughout the United States.

To shelter the fragile craft during stopovers on voyages from the company headquarters in Ohio to destinations in the Southeast, an enormous hangar structure was constructed behind the plant in East Gadsden. It was

The Goodyear Tire and Rubber Company erected a large hangar to shelter airships during overnight stops in Gadsden. *Gadsden Public Library*.

the first of its type to be constructed in the southern United States and was expected to be of considerable benefit to aviation and, ironically, a means of encouraging elected officials in Gadsden to build a modern airport to serve the city.

The huge aerial dock measured 200 feet in length, 75 feet in width and 76 feet in height and could accommodate an airship of the *Defender* type the company was constructing at the time. Christened by celebrated aviator Amelia Earhart in August 1929, *Defender* stretched 192 feet in length, had a capacity of 160,000 cubic feet of helium gas and was configured to carry eight passengers. According to local newspaper articles, excitement would fill the city whenever the new airship arrived at the plant.

Constructed to protect transient blimps during periods of inclement weather, the Gadsden blimp hangar once was used to protect the remains of one of the Goodyear airships destroyed because of inclement weather. On November 20, 1930, the Goodyear blimp *Vigilant* was en route to Atlanta, Georgia, to pick up P.W. Litchfield, president of the company, who had been attending a meeting of the board of directors of the U.S. Chamber of Commerce. Operating in thick fog near the community of Piedmont, Alabama, the blimp crashed into Oakey Mountain and was demolished.

Farmers in the vicinity observed the ship smash into a tree on top of the mountain. Miraculously, there were no injuries. The salvageable remains of *Vigilant* were transported to Gadsden for storage. Ironically, one year earlier, on November 29, 1929, *Vigilant* had been a featured attraction during the dedication ceremony of Lay Dam on the Coosa River, just downstream from Gadsden.

As the Goodyear fleet was modernized with new airships having increased performance and extended range, the hangar at the Gadsden plant soon became obsolete. Eventually, the building was used to store supplies of rubber and other products being used to manufacture automobile tires. In time, the Gadsden plant would earn the distinction of being the largest tire plant in the world, producing forty thousand tires daily.

Today, the sole remnant of the passing of a generation of airships that launched the concept of the aerial billboard is the concrete foundation of the enormous hangar that once sheltered the pride of the Goodyear fleet. Once the only structure of its type in the southern United States, the building was eventually demolished, closing a chapter in the unique and remarkable history of aviation in Alabama.

The Goodyear blimp *Vigilant* in Gadsden. *Gadsden Public Library.*

ARSENAL OF DEMOCRACY

When my brother and I built the first man-carrying flying machine we thought that we were introducing into the world an invention which would make further wars practically impossible.
—Orville Wright, 1917

TAYLOR FIELD:
THE BIRTHPLACE OF MILITARY AVIATION IN ALABAMA

Aircraft parked on the flight line of Maxwell Air Force Base at Montgomery are a testament to the sophistication and complexity of military aviation in the twenty-first century. Massive hangars built to shelter these multimillion-dollar investments in the nation's arsenal of democracy tower above the other structures that comprise this small city of more than ten thousand military and civilian personnel. Base Operations, the focal point of aerial activity on the base, is located near the convergence of the flight line and parking apron. Erected in the center of the circular drive leading to Base Operations, easily overlooked among the imposing structures nearby, is a modest stone monument. Etched into the face of the marker is the simple inscription: "On This Site in 1910 Stood the Hangar of the Flying School of the First Men to Fly: The Wright Brothers." This marker is the sole reminder of a one-hundred-acre cotton field that was the site of the nation's first civilian flying school and Alabama's first airfield. Equally significant, the

ON THIS SITE IN 1910
STOOD THE HANGAR
OF THE
FLYING SCHOOL OF THE
FIRST MEN TO FLY:
THE WRIGHT BROTHERS

The memorial commemorating the site of the flying school of the Wright brothers is located on Maxwell Air Force Base in Montgomery.

marker represents the convergence of flight training and military aviation in the state, a relationship that has endured for more than a century and produced thousands of aviation cadets for military service.

Despite the Wright brothers' peaceful intentions for their invention, the airplane would evolve into an effective tactical weapon during the First World War. As the United States began to mobilize its military forces to intervene in the war to end all wars, the Aviation Section of the Signal Corps was assigned the task of training five thousand aviators for service in the skies over Europe. With only two flying fields and fifty-five training aircraft in service when the United States entered the war, production of aircraft and construction of flying fields became an immediate priority.

In July 1917, Congress appropriated $640 million to fund the expansion of military aviation in the United States. Chief Signal Officer Brigadier General George O. Squire implemented a five-point plan to undertake the massive expansion of military airpower. The primary objectives of the plan included training an initial cadre of American aviators at existing Allied aviation training schools in Europe; expedited procurement of aircraft from

France; the creation of infrastructure needed to produce combat aircraft for American pilots at the front; the development of training planes for American aviators; and construction of a vast network of aviation training schools in the United States. Lieutenant Colonel Clinton G. Edgar, a graduate of Cornell University, was assigned the responsibility of selecting sites for construction of twenty-four primary and advanced flying fields in the United States.

Edgar formed a committee to travel throughout the country to inspect sites and negotiate for purchase or lease suitable parcels of land for the construction of flying fields. However, before the site selection could begin, a basic design for military flying fields needed to be developed. Using Langley Field, a military aviation facility located in Virginia, as a model, engineers created a standard design for a single-unit training airfield consisting of fifty-four buildings to accommodate one hundred aircraft, 150 student aviators and required support personnel. Situated on a one-square-mile section of land, buildings would be arranged in linear fashion along one side of the field. Level ground was essential, even though a slightly falling site, if available, could be utilized.

By the fall of 1917, potential sites in the northern United States were no longer being considered because of the potential for disruptions to flight training caused by inclement winter weather. Only sites in the southern and Pacific Coast states were to be evaluated. Like the Wright brothers before them, army inspectors recognized that the mild weather conditions and flat terrain of central Alabama made the area suitable for the operation of flying machines. At the invitation of Congressman Hubert Dent and Senator John H. Bankhead, a contingent of inspectors arrived in Alabama in November 1917. The inspection team first visited sites in Tuscaloosa before continuing to Montgomery, where a committee appointed by the mayor greeted them. The inspectors were given a tour of prospective sites that included the Kohn Place, where the Wright brothers established their aviation school, and other parcels of property available for lease to the government; the Randolph Place, located just south of Catoma Creek on Norman Bridge Road; the McGehee Place, near the Masonic Home; and the Ledyard Place, located five miles from the city on Wares Ferry Road. Eventually, an eight-hundred-acre tract of land located twelve miles southeast of Montgomery near the Pike Road community was selected as the site of one of fourteen primary training fields of the Aviation Section, United States Signal Corps.

In December 1917, workers began converting the rural farmland into a modern military airfield. Upon completion, the installation would consist of sixteen large hangars—engine and airframe repair shops, warehouses, hospital, living quarters and a swimming pool. Named for Captain Ralph L. Taylor of Stanford, Connecticut, a military aviator who lost his life in August 1917 in an aviation accident at Mineola Field, New York, Taylor Field was a model miniature city with every city convenience. Base personnel had access to telephones, electricity and indoor plumbing, luxuries that were not available to residents of the Pike Road community.

About two hundred aircraft were utilized in the training program at Taylor Field, including the Curtiss JN-4D. Affectionately known as the "Jenny," the JN-4D was powered by a ninety-horsepower, water-cooled OX-5 engine that produced a maximum horizontal flight speed of 75 miles per hour. The de Havilland DH-4 was also utilized by cadets at Taylor Field. Powered by a four-hundred-horsepower, water-cooled Liberty engine, the DH-4 could achieve a maximum speed of approximately 120 miles per hour.

Because the aircraft were not equipped with radios, students and instructors utilized hand signals to communicate. The flying field was divided into two sections: one side was used by cadets and their instructors, with the opposite side for cadets flying without the aid of an instructor. Individual aircraft were assigned a number that was displayed on the side of the fuselage to allow base personnel to manage flight operations at the field.

Before arriving at Taylor Field, cadets were required to complete courses in theory of flight, the operation and maintenance of aircraft engines, weather and other subjects at one of eight designated universities. During the first stage of primary flight training, cadets received about forty hours of flight training, initially accompanied by a flight instructor, to master the function of the flight controls and how to perform basic maneuvers. Cadets then progressed to the cross-country stage of training that consisted of three flights of a predetermined distance around a triangular course followed by a longer round-trip flight to a destination at least seventy-five miles from the point of departure. Rudimentary maps, nonexistent navigational aids and a lack of prepared landing fields made this phase one of the more challenging aspects of the training program.

The final phase of primary training consisted of instruction in acrobatics. Students learned to recover from stalls and spiral dives and to perform loops. After becoming proficient in these maneuvers, cadets practiced formation flying in groups of three to six aircraft. Successfully completing the Reserve Military Aviator test at the conclusion of primary training entitled the cadet to wear the wings of a military aviator. Graduates of

Established in December 1917, Taylor Field was established in the Pike Road community southeast of Montgomery. *AFHRA*.

The Curtiss JN-4 "Jenny" was utilized by cadets during primary training at Taylor Field. *Mark Pace Collection*.

Left: Standard equipment for military aviators at Taylor Field included a leather coat, gloves and flying helmet with goggles.

Below: The combination of inexperienced cadets and underpowered aircraft increased the potential for accidents. *Mark Pace Collection.*

primary schools would then be assigned to an advanced training base for instruction in fighter, bomber or reconnaissance aircraft before being assigned to a combat squadron.

The combination of inexperienced cadets and frail, underpowered aircraft often resulted in accidents. On June 4, 1918, Cadet George O. Mills was flying solo when a fire erupted in the engine compartment. Witnesses reported that Mills attempted to escape the flames by executing a side-slip maneuver and stopping the motor. He climbed onto the wing of the aircraft and held on to his seatbelt until the flames died away. While attempting to make his way back into the aircraft, the machine plunged into the earth, killing Mills instantly.

Not every accident was attributed to mechanical failures. Dashing young aviators from Taylor Field routinely performed aerial stunts over the home of local socialite Zelda Sayre. One of these performances resulted in tragedy when two aircraft crashed while competing for the attention of the ever-popular and attractive Sayre. Lieutenant Lincoln Weaver, who once proposed marriage to the young socialite, was severely injured in the accident. Sayre would later wed a young soldier by the name of F. Scott Fitzgerald, who was briefly assigned to Camp Sheridan in Montgomery.

Damaged aircraft were repaired in shops at Taylor Field or the Aviation Repair Depot in Montgomery. Mechanics were able to fabricate all wooden components of the airplane, including the propeller, wings and fuselage. Aircraft damaged beyond repair would be salvaged for serviceable parts to be used on other aircraft.

The November 1918 Armistice set into motion a rapid demobilization of the United States military forces. In April 1919, Taylor Field was decommissioned, although the property remained under government control until the end of the Second World War. As the nation prepared for a second world conflict two decades later, the establishment of flight training at Taylor Field would play a pivotal role in shaping the future of military aviation in Alabama.

From Cotton Fields to Airfields: Alabama's Aviation Training Bases

On the evening of December 29, 1940, President Franklin Roosevelt entered the Diplomatic Reception Room of the White House to deliver one of his legendary fireside chats, a radio broadcast that would reach millions of people across the nation and abroad. On this evening, the largest audience in broadcast history gathered in homes and other venues to hear the words of the president. As Roosevelt finalized the remarks that would be considered by future historians as one of the most important speeches in history, the skies over London were filled with aircraft of the German Luftwaffe, subjecting the civilian population to a night of terror during the worst aerial attack on that city since the onset of hostilities in Europe. To convince American citizens of the global threat posed by the German military, Roosevelt concluded his remarks with words that would be etched into the pages of history: "As President of the United States, I call for a national effort. I call for it in the name of this nation which we love and honor and are privileged and proud to serve. We must be the great arsenal of democracy."

As President Roosevelt spoke to the nation, Maxwell Field in Montgomery was the sole military aviation facility in Alabama. By the time the U.S. Congress voted to approve a declaration of war against the Germany, Italy and Japan on December 9, 1941, four additional bases would be operational in the state: Craig Field at Selma; Gunter Field in Montgomery; Napier Field at Dothan; and Barin Field, in Baldwin County. Two additional training bases would be added within two years with activation of the Tuskegee Army Air Field in Macon County and the Courtland Army Air Field in Lawrence County. The urgent need to train military aviators would also result in the recruitment of civilian operators, under contract with the Army Air Forces, to provide primary pilot training at local civilian airfields in Decatur, Tuscaloosa and Tuskegee. The Southeast Army Air Depot at Brookley Field in Mobile, established in 1939, provided logistical and maintenance support for army aviation facilities in the southeast United States, Puerto Rico and the Caribbean. The construction of military airfields in Alabama during the Second World War would transform thousands of acres of farmland, often former cotton fields, into small cities having populations numbering in the thousands.

The magnitude of training conducted in Alabama during the Second World War is best illustrated by the Southeast Army Air Forces Training Center located at Maxwell Field near Montgomery. Before the end of the war, more than 100,000 cadets completed training at Maxwell Field. Because so many potential pilots, navigators and bombardiers transitioned through the base, cadets adopted the slogan, "The road to Tokyo leads through Maxwell Field."

During the Second World War, military aviation training bases in Alabama became an integral component of the great arsenal of democracy. *AFHRA*.

More than 100,000 pilots, navigators and bombardiers attended training at Maxwell Field during the Second World War. *AFHRA.*

The wrap-around runway design at military air bases allowed uninterrupted flight training by eliminating lost time adjusting to changes in wind direction. *AFHRA.*

The need for pilots in a war that President Roosevelt believed would be won through superior air power created a sense of urgency in creating the network of training bases. In April 1941, the War Department issued final approval for the construction of an advanced pilot training school to be established in the Grimes community near the city of Dothan. Less than two months of time elapsed before construction of the base commenced. To accommodate the four hundred aircraft projected to be based at the facility, engineers developed a plan that included four paved runways, a concrete aircraft parking ramp, two large hangars and two hundred buildings to house military and support personnel. The base encompassed more than one thousand acres of land.

Working day and night, more than 1,500 workers labored to complete the project on schedule. During the peak of construction activity, fifty railroad cars filled with building materials arrived daily on two railroad spurs leading to the site. In October 1941, about three months since construction of the new airfield commenced, the first airplane landed on one of the recently completed runways. In a remarkable feat of coordination and effort, only six months elapsed from the first shovel full of dirt being turned until the December 1941 initiation of full-scale flight operations.

Even by current standards, construction of aviation training bases during the Second World War was an enormous task. Upon activation in 1940, the two-thousand-acre Selma Army Air Base, designated Craig Field, was the largest flying field in the United States. Comparatively, LaGuardia Airport in New York City, one of the largest civilian fields in the nation, consisted of six hundred acres. The landing field at Craig was about two miles in length and one mile in width, making it twice as large as the average military airfield in use at the time.

The Alabama Congressional delegation worked diligently to secure military installations and defense industries in Alabama during the war. Senator Lister Hill collaborated with community leaders to convince military officials to build training bases in Selma and Dothan, while the efforts of Congressman Frank Boykin resulted in the selection of Mobile over Tampa, Florida, as the location of the Southeastern Air Depot, which would employ nearly seventeen thousand workers during the war. The opportunity to secure good-paying jobs in a region that trailed other states in recovering from the financial Depression generated popular support for these installations among local populations.

The construction of training bases had an enormous impact on the communities where they were located. In early 1942, the community of

Left: The opportunity to create jobs in communities affected by the worldwide financial Depression generated popular local support of military aviation training bases in Alabama. *AFHRA*.

Below: During the Second World War, aviation training bases in Alabama were often commissioned within six months of the initiation of construction. *AFHRA*.

Opposite: With four thousand military and civilian personnel stationed at Courtland Army Air Field, the base was larger than the community in which it was located. *AFHRA*.

Courtland consisted of fewer than five hundred residents. In April of that year, officials of the Army Air Forces announced that a site near the town had been selected as the location of a new basic flight training school. The two-thousand-acre tract of land, known by residents as Shackleford Quarters, was a farming community whose primary source of income was derived from the cultivation of cotton. Following acquisition of the land, the U.S. Army Corps of Engineers began to transform the quiet farmland into a military flying school.

Initially projected to support a training capacity of five hundred students and three thousand military and civilian support personnel, the base required 5 million board feet of lumber to construct three hundred buildings on the facility. The runways and ramp areas contained enough concrete to build a road, twenty-two feet in width, between the cities of Muscle Shoals and Decatur, a distance of fifty miles. The airfield complex consisted of four asphalt runways situated in a wrap-around pattern that would allow takeoffs and landings to always be made into the prevailing wind. This design allowed for increased utilization of the facility regardless of prevailing surface wind conditions. The steel-reinforced concrete runways were the strongest of any of the thirty-five air bases of the Army Air Forces Eastern Training Center, poured to a thickness of eighteen inches to accommodate heavy bombardment aircraft.

On December 14, 1942, just six months and six days after initiation of construction, Courtland Army Air Field was activated. During the ceremonial raising of the American flag, Colonel C.P. West, commanding officer of the school, stated, "This post is being activated a year and seven days after the attack on Pearl Harbor. This school and all primary, basic, advanced and special schools in the Southeast and throughout the country are the answer that will mean victory for the Allies. Now let's go to work and do more than our share of the job."

At the peak of operations in 1944, four thousand military and civilian personnel were employed at Courtland Army Air Field. The military depended heavily on the local civilian population to operate an installation of this size. To secure sufficient labor to staff the multitude of support functions at the base, civilian personnel were recruited from small communities throughout Alabama. During 1944, more than eight hundred civilians were employed at the base.

Because of its remote location, recreational activities that included a bowling alley, theater, dances and United Service Organization shows were provided for base personnel. Sports also played a significant role in maintaining morale. Facilities for volleyball, basketball, track and field and gymnastics were provided, while softball, basketball and baseball teams were organized to compete against communities in North Alabama. The Basic Flyers, the base softball team competing in the Decatur League, won the championship during the 1944 season.

Perhaps the most notable military aviation training base constructed in Alabama during the Second World War was the Tuskegee Army Air Field. In compliance with the decision to accept African American cadets into its ranks in January 1941, officials of the Army Air Forces decided to maintain segregated training facilities despite protests from supporters of an integrated Armed Forces. Because Tuskegee Institute had previously established an aviation training program, representatives of the college petitioned officials of the Army Air Forces to locate the proposed facility in their area.

The training of African American pilots at Tuskegee originated in 1939 with the implementation of the Civilian Pilot Training Program. This program was designed to utilize the classrooms of American colleges and universities and the facilities of local flying schools to provide government funded flight instruction to civilians who would then be available for military service in the event of a national emergency. In Alabama, nine colleges participated in the training of civilian pilots.

With a loan provided by the Julius Rosenwald Fund, a philanthropic organization founded by the president of the Sears and Roebuck Company, 650 acres of land located three miles northeast of the Tuskegee campus was obtained for construction of a new flying field that would be named for Robert Russa Moton, a former president of Tuskegee Institute. In August 1941, the 66th Army Air Forces Flying Training Detachment, established to provide primary flight training for the first class of African American flight cadets in the history of the United States military, began operations.

Concurrent with the construction of Moton Field, the Army Air Corps approved the purchase of 1,600 acres of land located seven miles northwest of Tuskegee near the community of Chehaw. This land would be used for the construction of the Tuskegee Army Air Field to provide basic and advanced training to African American pilots of the U.S. Army Air Forces. Completed in 1942, the base became a temporary home to two hundred officers and three thousand enlisted personnel. Base facilities included a commissary, chapel, library, mess halls and barracks buildings. The base newspaper, the *Hawks Cry*, contained news of the war and attractions at the base theater. Performers such as Ella Fitzgerald, Cab Calloway and

Tuskegee Army Air Field was the only military facility in the United States to provide basic and advanced flight training for African American pilots. *AFHRA.*

Lena Horne provided musical entertainment for base personnel through the United Service Organization. Before being decommissioned in June 1946, more than one thousand aviators graduated from the training programs at Tuskegee Army Air Field.

In addition to the main training bases, more than thirty auxiliary landing fields were constructed in the state. With nearly four hundred training aircraft stationed at each main base, available runway facilities for takeoff and landing practice were severely limited. To reduce congestion, each main base was assigned as many as five auxiliary landing fields. After the war, many of these auxiliary landing fields were declared surplus property and the deeds transferred to local municipalities for use as civilian airports.

Following the end of the Second World War, military aviation training bases in Alabama were decommissioned almost as quickly as they had appeared only a few years earlier. By 1946, training activities at Courtland, Tuskegee, Napier Field in Dothan and Gunter Field in Montgomery had been terminated. The Southeast Army Air Depot at Brookley Field in Mobile would continue to support military aviation operations until 1966, when it was closed because of a reduction in federal military spending. Craig Air Force Base in Selma closed in September 1977 because of budget constraints and a reduction in the number of pilots being trained following the withdrawal of the United States military from Southeast Asia. During thirty-seven years in operation, more than thirty thousand pilots were trained at the base.

Even though the histories of these bases have been recorded in military records and other publications, their true historical significance is more difficult to articulate. The military and civilian personnel who served at the bases, as well as the communities that supported them, were critical to their success. In his 1945 address to the first advanced flying school class to graduate following the Allied victory in Europe, Colonel Charles B. Stewart, commanding officer of Napier Field, stated, "Five years ago, this patch of country was devoted solely to agriculture and pasture land. In less than a year, a remarkable change had taken place. The United States was arming against a definite and terrible threat to her security. This land had miraculously turned into a flying field dedicated to making better pilots than those in the Luftwaffe. That it succeeded in its task is proven by written history. All of those who had a part in the life of this field will feel regret at its passing. However, they can at the same time be tremendously proud of the work accomplished and the part played in winning the greatest of all wars."

In March 1910, the promise of short winters, a mild climate and flat farmland convinced the Wright brothers to establish the nation's first civilian flying school in Alabama. Less than a decade later, the army constructed one of the earliest military aviation training fields in the state for similar reasons. In Alabama, the Wright brothers and the military found an ideal environment for training aviators to operate flying machines. More important than climate or terrain, they discovered a state deeply committed in its support of aviation and the development of military airpower, a level of commitment that will ensure the aviation legacy of Alabama during the second century of powered flight.

SILENT WINGS OVER ALABAMA

Before Orville and Wilbur Wright first achieved powered flight in a heavier-than-air machine over the sand dunes of Kitty Hawk, North Carolina, humans dreamed of emulating the birds that appeared to soar effortlessly through the air. Although the earliest designs of flying machines date back to the drawings of Leonardo da Vinci in the fifteenth century, it was not until the nineteenth century that Otto Lilienthal, a mechanical engineer from Germany, made the first controlled gliding flights in a craft of his own design. Lilienthal began his gliding experiments in 1891 near his home in Berlin. Initially, the flights lasted only seconds, but by 1894, he had begun experimenting with advanced designs that allowed him to extend his glides to distances of more than seven hundred feet. Prior to his death in an accident in 1896, Lilienthal had conducted more than two thousand successful glides.

Inspired by the fights of Otto Lilienthal, other early aviation experimenters began designing unpowered flying machines known as gliders. In 1902, Orville and Wilbur Wright utilized a glider to develop the three-axis control system critical to the successful flight of their powered machine the following year.

By 1929, aviation enthusiasts in the United States were advocating the use of gliders as a safe and inexpensive alternative to flight training in powered airplanes. Training in a glider allowed student pilots to concentrate on the fundamentals of aircraft control without having to be concerned about complicated engine and fuel systems. After becoming proficient in basic aerial maneuvers, students completed their training in powered aircraft, a more cost-effective method because of the lower operating and maintenance expense of the glider.

In Germany, the use of gliders for training pilots had become a necessity. In accordance with the provisions of the Treaty of Versailles that was ratified by the belligerent nations following the First World War, Germany was forced to deactivate its air force and destroy its remaining powered warplanes. Consequently, German aviation enthusiasts acquired considerable skill in the development and production of unpowered aircraft. By 1919, glider clubs had begun to appear throughout Germany, and the sport of flying gliders became a popular pastime. Even though participants viewed their sport as an enjoyable hobby, officials within the German military considered glider clubs to be a readily available source to recruit pilot candidates should a reconstructed German air force become a reality.

When Adolf Hitler became chancellor of Germany in January 1933, that dream became a reality. Hitler created a Ministry of Aviation that immediately placed civilian glider clubs into the *Deutsche Luftsport Verbund*, a subsidiary of the air ministry. Large black swastikas, the emblem of the Nazi Party, adorned the tail sections of German sport gliders. What had been an enjoyable hobby became a rigidly controlled state-supported activity with the stated goal of producing pilots for the powered aircraft combat squadrons of the new German Luftwaffe. In March 1935, after defiantly announcing that Germany no longer considered itself bound by the provisions of the Treaty of Versailles, Hitler shocked the nations of the world by unveiling his new aerial armada. Less than five years later, he unleashed *blitzkrieg* attacks against Poland, Belgium, Luxembourg and the Netherlands. A significant aspect of these early military campaigns was the innovative use of the glider as a transport for troops and equipment, converting what was once a means of recreation into an instrument of war.

The use of gliders in the successful campaigns of German forces in Belgium and the Balkans convinced military officials in the United States to consider the use of gliders as a tactical weapon. As the probability of American involvement in the war in Europe increased, Major General Henry H. "Hap" Arnold, chief of the Army Air Forces, authorized the development of military gliders capable of transporting personnel and weapons to seize objectives that could not be reached by conventional means.

Officials of the Army Air Forces faced a dilemma: development of a glider training program without the benefit of military expertise in this area. To initiate the training of glider pilots as rapidly as possible, General Arnold directed contracts to be negotiated with civilian glider schools for

Initially, cadets of the 18th Army Air Forces Glider Training Detachment utilized civilian gliders during training. *AFHRA*.

the development of a training program for military glider pilots. The Elmira Area Soaring Corporation (EASC) of Elmira, New York, and the Lewis School of Aeronautics in Lockport, Illinois, were the first of two civilian organizations selected to train military glider pilots.

Originally formed to promote the sport of soaring, the EASC provided glider training for civilian pilots. Because harsh winter weather conditions in the Northeast made it difficult to conduct glider training for several months each year, military officials informed EASC of the necessity to relocate its operations to an area of the country with more favorable weather conditions.

Representatives of EASC visited several areas in the Southeast to locate a suitable site for the establishment of a flying field and training center. In the spring of 1942, EASC officials arrived in Mobile, Alabama. The site being considered for the relocation of the glider school was the new Mobile municipal airport, Bates Field. When officials visited the airport, three runways, each about five thousand feet in length, had just been constructed. After officials of EASC completed their inspection and returned to Elmira, the War Department requested an immediate clearance to utilize the

Mobile Municipal Airport as a glider school with training to begin on July 6, 1942. Designated the 18th Army Air Forces Glider Training Detachment, the elementary/advanced training school became one of only two such programs in existence in the United States.

Work began immediately on construction of facilities, improvements to the airport and preparation of auxiliary landing fields. Like other training airfields being built during the early days of the war, cadets arriving at Mobile found the facility in various stages of construction. Cadets lived in tents while eating their meals in an open mess hall, an arrangement that caused the morale of the cadets to fluctuate with the weather. Hangar facilities used in maintaining tow aircraft and gliders were leased from civilian operators at the airport.

Training at Mobile consisted of a four-week program to produce pilots qualified to operate gliders in the various types of towed and soaring flight, both night and day, and to be qualified to service gliders in the field. Cadets received seventy-two hours of ground instruction in meteorology, soaring technique, aerodynamics, air towing, maintenance, instruments and navigation. Concurrent with ground instruction, the cadets received thirty hours of flight training that included launching the glider by winch, auto and airplane tow. Emphasis was placed on spot landing proficiency. Additionally, cadets were to be qualified in assembly, servicing and maintenance of the gliders and towing gear. Upon graduation, cadets would be promoted to the rank of staff sergeant and awarded the rating of glider pilot.

Initially, the Mobile detachment was authorized the use of five Stinson L1-A single-engine aircraft and six Douglas C-47 twin-engine aircraft for use in towing gliders. Additionally, thirty-six training gliders, ranging from single-place sport aircraft to thirteen-place troop and cargo transport gliders, were to be assigned to Mobile. Initially, only six gliders and seven tow aircraft were immediately available. After six weeks of operations, the Mobile facility employed 107 civilian administrative and maintenance personnel, tow pilots and flight instructors.

The airspace around Bates Field was divided into three areas; the first section was designated for tow aircraft to pull the glider to the required altitude. The tow aircraft and glider then crossed into the second area, where the pilot of the tow aircraft would signal the pilot of the glider to release the towline. The tow aircraft then flew into the third area to descend for landing. Gliders were routinely towed to altitudes of six thousand to eight thousand feet. To guard against low ambient temperatures at these altitudes, cadets wore heavy flight jackets and trousers. After completing required in-flight

In addition to flight training in gliders, cadets received instruction in military infantry tactics. *AFHRA*.

A Stinson L-1A aircraft with the pilots of multiple gliders practicing a formation tow from Bates Field in Mobile. *AFHRA*.

Because of a shortage of gliders for training, civilian airplanes were converted into training aircraft by removal of the engine.

maneuvers, the cadets executed a figure-eight maneuver that allowed them to lose altitude and still maintain proximity to the landing field.

The combination of inexperienced pilots and the accelerated pace of the training program occasionally resulted in accidents. During one training flight, a student and instructor were conducting a high-speed dive in a glider when the plastic canopy covering the flight deck separated from the aircraft. Uninjured, the student pilot decided to loosen his safety belt in the event he needed to parachute to safety. After loosening the belt, the force of the slipstream blew the student out of the glider. Thinking that the student must have a good reason for parachuting to safety, the flight instructor elected to follow. Descending under their parachutes, the student and instructor watched the glider descend and land virtually undamaged in a tree.

The most notable graduate of the 18th Army Air Forces Glider Training Detachment was Flight Officer Samuel Fine. After completing the course at Mobile, Fine attended advanced training on the Waco CG-4A combat glider at Stuttgart, Arkansas. Upon graduation, Fine was assigned to the 316th Troop Carrier Group, becoming one of the first American glider pilots to be sent overseas. On July 9, 1943, Fine was among a group of thirty volunteer American military glider pilots who participated in Operation

Husky, a joint American and British airborne and amphibious invasion of Sicily. During the mission, Fine became the first American to land a glider in combat during the Second World War. Even though he was wounded three times in the fierce battle that took place after he landed his glider behind enemy lines, Fine continued to fight in the best tradition of the British Glider Pilot Regiment to which he was attached. Because of his heroism, Fine received the Army Air Forces Air Medal.

Military planners originally anticipated a need to train six thousand pilots. By 1943, the shortage of training gliders and tow aircraft resulted in a massive backlog of pilots awaiting training. Furthermore, the logistical difficulties of transporting replacement combat gliders to overseas theaters of operations created extensive delays in serviceable gliders being available for use in combat. These factors eventually forced a reevaluation of the glider program.

Approval of the "Glider Pilot Training Objective and the Disposition of Excess Glider Personnel" directive in 1943 established a revised training schedule that created a surplus of more than five thousand pilots. Because of the reduction in the training requirement, officials of the Army Air Forces directed all basic glider training schools to be closed within thirty days. Personnel of the 18th Army Air Forces Glider Training Detachment were advised that all contracts were to be canceled and operations terminated by March 15, 1943.

Curtailment of pilot training marked the beginning of the end of the military glider program. In contrast to other technological developments during the war, the combat glider had no precedent. These aircraft were the result of the necessity to transport large quantities of equipment and personnel directly into battle. The selection of Mobile as the site of one of the first military glider training schools was unique in the histories of aviation, the state of Alabama and the United States military. Although new technologies consigned this program to history, the state of Alabama maintains a legacy of attracting new and innovative aviation programs. As America turned its attention to space, this legacy continued, as the Marshall Space Flight Center served an integral role in the development and operation of the space shuttle, the most advanced glider ever designed.

Extraordinary Events

Unique and unusual occurrences represent an important chapter in the history of aviation in Alabama and in the lives of those aviators who participated in these extraordinary events.

The Aviator Who Fell from the Sky

Motorists passing Bud Newell Park on Brooklane Drive in Hueytown seldom take notice of the marble monument located only a short distance from the local community center. A chain link fence that surrounds the monument adds a sense of protection and permanence to the setting. Erected almost one hundred years ago, the memorial was placed on the site where a young aviator lost his life during the formative years of aviation.

Born in Jasper, Alabama, in 1898, Dennis Orlando Gabbert became fascinated with the concept of flight as a young man. After graduating from high school, he became an employee of the Ensley Division of the Tennessee Coal and Iron Company. In April 1923, Dennis Gabbert enlisted in the 114th Observation Squadron, Alabama National Guard based at Roberts Field in Birmingham. During his three-year term of enlistment, he received training as a pilot in the Curtiss JN-4 "Jenny" aircraft operated by the squadron and earned satisfactory evaluations from his flight instructor, Asa Duncan. As the end of his three-year enlistment period approached, he made the decision to leave the military to pursue a career in the emerging aviation industry, a venture that would begin and end in tragedy.

On April 7, 1926, Gabbert and fellow aviator Roy Samson Dungan of Fairfield, Alabama, were piloting a military surplus Curtiss "Jenny" over Amory, Mississippi. Dungan, who began his aviation career making balloon ascensions and parachute jumps, purchased the tandem-seat aircraft to tour the American Southeast, selling rides to residents of the rural communities predominant throughout the region. The fuselage of the aircraft was adorned with product slogans to entice local merchants to take advantage of the unique opportunity to participate in a new age of aerial advertising. Operating from a local farm field, the aviators soon captured the imagination of residents and business owners.

Before departing for their next engagement near Little Rock, Arkansas, Gabbert and Dungan decided to make a final flight over the Amory community. Returning to land, their machine collided with a tree that bordered the field. Seated in the front pilot position, Roy Dungan was killed instantly, while Dennis Gabbert, occupying the rear seat, narrowly escaped death but suffered serious injuries in the accident.

Less than seven weeks after surviving the crash that claimed the life of his former friend and colleague, Dennis Gabbert and his new business partner, George Suel Byess, climbed into another surplus "Jenny" they intended to purchase from local aviator O.W. McDaniel. After making repairs to the machine, Gabbert and Byess planned to make a test flight from a makeshift flying field near Bessemer before finalizing the purchase.

Driving along the Bessemer Road, Clara Wright, accompanied by her sister and nephew, observed the airplane carrying Gabbert and Byess flying overhead. As she continued to watch, the aircraft appeared to begin a series of twisting and turning maneuvers that Wright attributed to the pilots doing fancy tricks. Suddenly, as Wright and her companions continued to watch, the airplane began to rapidly lose altitude. Believing that the machine would return to level flight at any moment, she soon realized that something was dreadfully wrong as the airplane continued its steep descent. The airplane impacted the ground with a deafening crash three hundred yards in front of her automobile. Rushing to the site, her car was the third to arrive at the accident scene. In a newspaper article the next day, Wright recalled, "When we got there, the aircraft was one blasting flame. Two men were sitting upright in the cockpit but were burned beyond recognition. One of them still held the operating lever in his hand. Fortunately, they had been killed instantly when the plane hit the ground." She concluded the interview by declaring that the accident was the most awful thing she had ever experienced.

An unidentified individual seated in the Curtiss JN-4 aircraft that would subsequently claim the life of Dennis Orlando Gabbert.

Two stumps projecting upward on the spot where the airplane fell penetrated the fuselage and ruptured the fuel tank. Covered in gasoline, the machine erupted into flames that burned with intense fury for about twenty minutes. Within moments of the crash, an estimated three hundred automobiles arrived on the scene, parked so tightly along the highway that police officers were forced to clear a path for an ambulance to reach the victims. A fire department truck was called but arrived too late to provide any assistance.

Within twenty-four hours of the accident, the remains of Dennis Orlando Gabbert were interred at the Samaria Baptist Church Cemetery in Jasper. The Walker County *Mountain Eagle* newspaper reported that an impressive funeral and burial service was conducted as flowers were dropped on the grave site from aircraft flying overhead. The headstone that adorns the grave of the young aviator is inscribed with a simple statement of fact: "This box contains the ashes of Dennis and the plane in which he fell and was burned to death."

Rosalie Gabbert, mother of the young aviator, memorialized her son by erecting a monument on the site where he perished. During the dedication service, aviators of the 106th Observation Squadron from Roberts Field circled their airplanes overhead, dropping flowers on the assembled crowd below. The Police Department Band of Birmingham played a hymn as the

The remains of Dennis Orlando Gabbert were interred at the Samaria Baptist Church Cemetery in Jasper.

The monument memorializing Dennis Orlando Gabbert is located on Brookline Drive adjacent to Bud Newall Park in Hueytown.

marble monument, adorned with a medallion photograph of the flier seated in his airplane, was unveiled. The service closed with a song written by Rosalie Gabbert and performed by the McDonald Quartet.

Almost a century has passed since the tragic accident that claimed the life of Dennis Gabbert. The ravages of time and the indignities perpetrated by vandals have taken a toll on the monument and the memory of the young aviator. The medallion photograph of Dennis Gabbert, stolen many years ago, arouses a profound sense of loss for a young man seeking his place in the fledging aviation industry, a profession terribly unforgiving of carelessness, incapacity or neglect.

The words etched into the marble stone of the monument, penned by a grieving mother, preserve for all time the memory of her son:

> *Whose plane fell from among the clouds carrying his manly form to this spot of earth. His soul went to God who gave it. With the crushing plane, his manly form came whirling to the ground. He fought so hard to save his life but uttered not one sound as the angels they did come and take him home to God. All we have left is his precious form beneath the sod.*

THE MIRACLE OF FLIGHT 002

The polished aluminum skin of the Eastern Air Lines Douglas DC-2 reflected the soft glow of the full moon on the night of October 18, 1938, as the large twin-engine aircraft sat motionless on the macadam parking ramp of Gunter Field, the Montgomery Municipal Airport. In the small two-story brick terminal building nearby, eleven passengers waited patiently to board Flight 002, overnight service from New Orleans, Louisiana, to Newark, New Jersey, with stops in Montgomery, Atlanta and other cities along the route. Scheduled to depart at 10:40 p.m., the DC-2 and its passengers would soon be airborne for the one-hour flight to Atlanta.

Entering service with Eastern Air Lines in 1934, the Douglas DC-2 represented a revolutionary advancement in air travel. The sleek fourteen-passenger, twin-engine, all-metal design provided significant improvements in reliability, economy, passenger comfort and speed as compared to other aircraft of the period. The DC-2 was among the first group of aircraft to be identified as the Great Silver Fleet, an advertising theme created to promote the safety and luxury of travel on Eastern Air Lines.

Flight 002, a Douglas DC-2 aircraft operated by Eastern Air Lines, crashed shortly after takeoff from Gunter Field in Montgomery. *ALAMY.*

In command of Flight 002, Captain John David Hissong had been employed by Eastern for four years. Hissong began his aviation career as an airmail pilot operating open-cockpit bi-planes constructed of wood and fabric on the Pueblo, Colorado, to Amarillo, Texas, segment of the transcontinental airmail route. An experienced pilot, Hissong was no stranger to in-flight emergencies. In December 1933, the thirty-four-year-old aviator was flying over the rural community of Watrous, New Mexico, when the engine of his Fokker Super Universal aircraft suddenly erupted in flames. Hissong was able to make an emergency landing and remove the pouches of mail before the aircraft was completely consumed by the raging fire.

After boarding passengers in Montgomery, Captain Hissong and co-pilot Clyde Russell began their preparations for takeoff. In the darkened cabin, flight steward Frank Gibbs conducted a final check to ensure that all passengers were comfortable with their seatbelts secured for takeoff. As the aircraft proceeded to the departure runway on this fall evening, the passengers settled in for what they expected to be a routine flight to Atlanta.

After an uneventful takeoff, the seasoned travelers began to unfasten their seatbelts in anticipation of the steward making his way through the cabin to distribute bottles of Coca-Cola and, for additional comfort, a piece of chewing gum to relieve the discomfort in their ears because of altitude changes in the unpressurized cabin.

As the DC-2 climbed through an altitude of 1,400 feet, Captain Hissong steered the aircraft in a gradual turn to an easterly course to Atlanta. Back at the airport, family and friends of the passengers watched as the aircraft appeared to grow smaller as it climbed into the night sky. Suddenly, a sense of horror swept over the group as the aluminum skin of the aircraft, polished to a mirror-like finish, began to reflect a streak of bright-orange flame enveloping the right engine.

Onboard the aircraft, Frank Gibbs had unfastened his seatbelt to begin serving the passengers when, without warning, the aircraft began to shake violently. Peering through a passenger window, he was startled to observe flames in the vicinity of the right engine. Gibbs recalled, "Then came a sickening jolt as the motor fell off the ship and the right wing flew up and the left wing dropped crazily." Reporting on the event the next day, an article in the *Montgomery Advertiser* newspaper quoted a source who stated, "Tense white knuckles gripped the backs of the seats as passengers braced themselves for the crash they knew was coming."

Within seconds, flames began to enter the cockpit. Expecting the aircraft to explode should the fire reach the fuel tanks, Hissong first attempted to turn back to land at the airport. He quickly realized, however, that the aircraft was rapidly becoming uncontrollable, making a return to the airport impossible. With the fuselage on fire and one engine missing from the aircraft, Captain Hissong decided to attempt a landing in a small field located one mile north of the Montgomery Atlanta Highway. Suffering burns to his hands and arms, Hissong knew that he had to maintain control of the aircraft for the passengers to have any chance of survival.

According to copilot Clyde Russell, "Captain Hissong cut the gas off from the motor. He attempted to turn and had completed about one-half of the turn toward the airport when the right motor, damaged by the flames, separated from the aircraft. Hissong jerked his left wing up to a flying position and headed for a clearing on the ground below. As the aircraft continued to descend, Hissong could barely discern the terrain even though the aircraft landing lights were illuminated." Before the airplane touched down, one passenger reported that he could see the fuel tank in the right wing where the metal skin had melted away.

Passengers would later report that the touchdown was so smooth that they did not realize the aircraft was on the ground until it impacted a tree, shearing off the right wing. As the burning aircraft skidded to a stop, Frank Gibbs began guiding passengers to safety through the rear entry door. After exiting the aircraft, he realized that Hissong and Russell remained trapped on the flight deck. Assisted by passengers, Gibbs returned to the flaming inferno to pull the pilots from the wreckage. Within minutes, the aircraft was completely engulfed in flames.

Although injured, passenger J.V. Connolly, general manager of Hearst Newspapers who was traveling to New York, made his way across the cotton field and climbed a barbed-wire fence to reach a farmhouse to telephone his office with a flash report of the accident. In his report, Connolly affirmed, "The heroism and fine work of the pilot were beyond description." Regarding his fellow passengers, he acknowledged, "All were great sportsmen, and none lost his nerve."

Following the arrival of fire trucks and ambulances, passengers were transported by automobile to a Montgomery hotel. Because their luggage had been destroyed in the post-crash fire, a Montgomery merchant opened his clothing store at 2:00 a.m. to provide much-needed necessities. Within five hours of their narrow escape, the passengers were offered seats on the 3:30 a.m. train to Atlanta. However, the more resilient members of the group decided to remain overnight to board another Eastern flight the following day.

As news of the successful emergency landing became public, Governor Bibb Graves suggested that proper recognition must be found for Captain Hissong for what he termed the performance of an aeronautical miracle. The governor of Georgia, whose son was a passenger on the flight, also praised the heroic performance of the pilot. Hissong refused to take credit for his courage and resourcefulness in saving the lives of his passengers. He emphatically stated that any other pilot would have reacted in the same manner in a similar situation. Hissong also gave credit to his fellow crewmembers: "Without the aid of Clyde Russell and Frank Gibbs, we could not have landed safely." He insisted that Russell and Gibbs be included in all press photographs.

Because Flight 002 was transporting 297 pounds of airmail, Captain Hissong received the Airmail Flyers Medal of Honor. Presented by Postmaster General Jesse M. Donaldson on October 4, 1948, on behalf of President Harry Truman, Hissong became the tenth and final recipient of the medal. The citation of the award read:

For extraordinary valor and achievement while piloting air mail plane NC 13735 on a flight from New Orleans to New York on the night of October 18, 1938. Soon after takeoff from the intermediate stop at Montgomery, Alabama for the flight to Atlanta, Georgia extreme

101

vibrations occurred in the right engine leading to progressive failure of its component parts. A fire of intense heat ignited by escaping gasoline and oil enveloped the engine and right wing and progressed toward the cabin. The engine burned from its fittings and dropped from the plane. The pilot, with great skill and courage, manipulated the controls to compensate for loss of the engine and burning wing, kept the plane aloft until dwellings were cleared, and then landed in the darkness without the landing gear in such manner that, although the burning wing was sheared off by contact with a tree, there was no impact. The passengers were freed from the plane a few seconds before it was entirely consumed. Besides three members of the plane crew, there were eleven passengers who earnestly say that they are indebted for their lives to the courage of Pilot Hissong, who alone was injured by minor burns.

One newspaper editorial described the successful emergency landing of Eastern Flight 002 as a new epic in the annals of air transportation, while other reporters proclaimed the survival of the passengers to be a miracle. Captain Hissong could not depend on a miracle to save the passengers of Flight 002 that fateful night. The real miracle was the skill, judgment and experience of John David Hissong that prevented a terrible ordeal from becoming a tragedy.

AN UNEXPLAINED ENCOUNTER

During the predawn hours of July 24, 1948, a twin-engine Eastern Air Lines DC-3 passenger aircraft was cruising at an altitude of five thousand feet on a route from Houston, Texas, to Atlanta, Georgia. The night sky was clear with the moon four days past full, illuminating the silvery aluminum skin of the aircraft through a thin layer of clouds overhead. In the dimly lit passenger cabin, only one of the twenty passengers remained awake at the early hour of 2:45 a.m. as the flight passed twenty miles to the west of Montgomery. The steady drone of the Pratt and Whitney engines provided a sense of security for the sleeping passengers as their metal cocoon traversed the night sky.

In command of the flight, Captain Clarence Childs was a former military aviator who had completed a tour of duty with the Air Transport Command during the Second World War. Copilot John Whitted was also a former military pilot who had served as a crewmember on Boeing B-29 Superfortress bombardment aircraft in the Pacific Theater of combat. Both were regarded as cautious and conservative aviators by their peers at Eastern Air Lines.

In the cockpit of the DC-3, the instrument lights were dimmed to a dull red glow to allow the pilots an unrestricted view of the world below. Captain Chiles gently manipulated the flight controls to prevent any sudden movements of the airplane that might disturb the sleeping passengers. To the south of their route of flight, the aviators observed an area of rain showers that did not appear to pose a hazard to the flight.

Sitting on the right side of the cockpit, Whitted continued to gaze out his window as the captain steered the DC-3 aircraft through the night sky. Suddenly, he noticed what looked to be a cylindrical object emerging from the distant squall line. Initially, he believed it to be one of the new jet-powered aircraft being evaluated by the military because of the bright glow emitted from the rear of the vehicle. However, the object did not appear to have wings or an empennage like a conventional aircraft.

Alerting Captain Chiles, both pilots continued to maintain visual contact with the object. In his official statement filed after the encounter, Whitted stated, "The object was cigar-shaped and appeared to be about three times

On July 24, 1948, the pilots of an Eastern Airlines DC-3 aircraft reported an encounter with an unidentified flying object in the night sky near Montgomery. *State Library and Archives of Florida.*

the circumference of a Boeing B-29 Superfortress fuselage and had two rows of windows, an upper and a lower. The windows were square, very large and appeared to emit a bright white light that seemed to be caused by some type of combustion."

The official statement of Captain Chiles was virtually identical in describing the craft: "It was clear there were no wings present and that it was powered by some jet or other type of power. Out of the rear end came an orange-red exhaust that extended back by about the same distance as the object's length. There were two rows of windows, an upper and lower deck. A very bright light was glowing from inside the windows. Underneath the ship, there was a blue glow of light."

The object seemed to be moving in the same direction as their aircraft at approximately the same altitude. Chiles recalled, "We veered to the left and it passed about 700 feet to our right and about 700 feet above us. Then, as if the pilot had seen us and wanted to avoid us, it pulled up with a tremendous burst of flame out of its rear and zoomed up into the clouds." Both Chiles and Whitted continued to observe the object for about ten seconds.

Immediately after the encounter, Captain Chiles made his way into the cabin section of the aircraft to determine if any of the passengers had observed anything unusual. One passenger, Charles McKelvie of Columbus, Ohio, had been awake during the encounter. During a subsequent interview with the Associated Press, McKelvie stated, "I was sitting on the right side of the plane. I suddenly saw this strange, eerie streak out of my window. I observed no shape or form. It was very intense, not like lightning or anything I had ever seen."

Immediately after landing in Atlanta, Chiles and Whitted reported the sighting to local authorities. The following day, the pilots completed extensive interviews conducted by personnel from Project Sign, the first official group within the U.S. Air Force responsible for investigating sightings of unidentified flying objects. During the interview, both Chiles and Whitted were asked to provide a drawing depicting the unidentified object. Investigators agreed that the drawings provided by both crew members were remarkably similar in detail.

Once the interview concluded, investigators created a map depicting the possible trajectory of the object. The map indicated that the object should have passed over Macon, Georgia, if it maintained an easterly track from the point of the sighting by Childs and Whitted. Searching for indications of unusual activity along this projected path, investigators were surprised

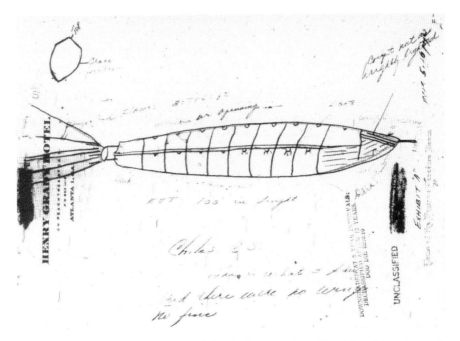

A drawing provided by pilot Clarence Chiles depicts the unidentified flying object observed near Montgomery.

to discover reports filed by personnel at Robbins Air Force Base near Macon. The reports described the existence of an extremely bright white light moving at a high rate of speed over the base on the same night as the Montgomery encounter.

Investigators were intrigued to note that the Montgomery sighting occurred less than one hundred miles south of Florence, Alabama, where, in July 1947, the *Florence Times* newspaper published the article "Have Flying Saucers Come to the Shoals Area?" The report included multiple eyewitness reports of unidentified objects observed over the cities of Florence, Sheffield and Muscle Shoals. One month later, two pilots flying overhead the community of Bethel in Wilcox County, located fifty miles southwest of Montgomery, reported a huge wingless object that crossed in front of their aircraft. As it was silhouetted against the evening sky, the pilots were unable to identify any wings, motors or jet exhaust. Even though they attempted to follow the object, it quickly outdistanced the 170-mile-per-hour speed of their aircraft.

It did not take long for news of the Chiles-Whitted encounter to capture the attention of the public. On the morning following the sighting, the headline of the *Atlanta Constitution*, a daily newspaper not inclined to publish sensational or unsubstantiated stories, proclaimed, "Atlanta Pilots Report Wingless Sky Monster." News agencies throughout the United States quickly picked up the story.

According to U.S. Air Force captain Edward Ruppelt of the Air Technical Intelligence Center, the report by Chiles and Whtted and other sightings in 1947 and 1948 convinced personnel of Project Sign to forward a highly classified document, *Estimate of the Situation*, to Hoyt S. Vandenberg, air force chief of staff. The report included incidents reported by multiple witnesses who observed wingless, cigar-shaped objects emitting blue or bright white lights. The report concluded that the encounter by two experienced airline pilots added to the concern relating to the presence of strange craft of unknown technology operating in the skies over the United States.

After reviewing the classified *Estimate of the Situation* report, Vandenburg rejected the findings because of his belief that the evidence was insufficient to support its conclusions. According to Captain Ruppelt, the report was subsequently declassified and destroyed. Subsequent studies by air force and civilian researchers concluded that the object observed by Childs and Whitted was a meteor, noting that the sighting occurred during a period of increased celestial activity. In 1959, the air force officially closed its investigation of the incident.

More than seven decades have passed since the sighting of an unidentified object in the predawn darkness over Montgomery, Alabama. The Chiles-Whitted Encounter, as the incident is widely known, remains one of the most controversial sightings ever recorded. Although officials of the U.S. Air Force closed their investigation into the event, civilian researchers still consider the sighting to be unexplained. As Robert Ripley, the renowned promoter of the mysterious and unexplained would suggest, readers can believe it or not!

THE LOST SQUADRON

On a small hill overlooking the hallowed grounds of the Oakwood Cemetery Annex in Montgomery, seventy-eight headstones are aligned with military precision to memorialize the lives and sacrifices of Royal Air Force cadets who perished during flight training in Montgomery during the Second World War. Nestled among their comrades in arms are the graves of seven young men who, like their fellow cadets, did not die in combat, but ultimately gave their full measure of devotion to the country and people they loved. The lives and dreams of these seven young men would come to a tragic end on the same night in May 1942, their deaths occurring in one of the worst aviation tragedies to occur in Alabama during the Second World War.

In the spring of 1942, Gunter Field in Montgomery was the most active basic training airfield in Alabama. One of four phases of training for military aviators, the basic phase consisted of instruction in aerobatics, maneuvering the aircraft by reference to flight instruments, formation flying involving multiple aircraft, cross-country navigation and night operations. Cadets completing the basic flying course would be assigned to an advanced training base to transition to single-engine fighter or multi-engine transport or bomber aircraft.

During the peak of operations in 1944, more than four hundred training aircraft were based at Gunter Field. Combined with the advanced pilot training operations at nearby Maxwell Field, the skies over Montgomery

During the Second World War, British and French aviation cadets were trained at Tuscaloosa, Montgomery and Dothan.

were described as the most congested airspace in the world. In 1942, Gunter Field became one of only two locations in the United States to provide basic flight training to British and French cadets.

At Gunter and other basic training fields, cadets were introduced to the Vultee BT-13 Valiant, an aircraft known as the "Vultee Vibrator" because of the excessive vibration and noise produced by the massive 450-horsepower Pratt and Whitney Wasp engine that propelled the aircraft through the air at a maximum speed of 180 miles per hour. The aircraft utilized a tandem seating arrangement in which the flight instructor normally occupied the rear pilot position, with the student situated in front. For cadets, the transition from the slow, docile training aircraft flown during the primary phase of training into the more advanced, higher-performance aircraft utilized in basic flying training was demanding and potentially dangerous. The combination of intensive training schedules and inexperienced pilots operating high-performance aircraft drastically increased the potential for accidents. During the predawn hours of May 21, 1942, these factors would combine to tragically claim seven lives in a war being fought on a distant continent.

As the sun began to set on that fateful afternoon, a flight of thirty-five aircraft operated by pilot cadets from the United Kingdom departed Gunter Field on a cross-country navigation training mission. Even though nine flight instructors accompanied selected students on the flight, most of the cadets were flying without the assistance of a more experienced pilot.

The formation of aircraft was scheduled to fly a direct course to Crestview, Florida, to refuel before proceeding to Mobile, Alabama, and returning to Gunter Field. The last two segments of the flight would be flown in darkness as part of the training requirements. The first leg of the flight was completed without difficulty, with all aircraft arriving at Crestview on schedule. After delaying for several hours to service their aircraft and have dinner, the British cadets departed for Mobile. The flight plan directed the flight to overfly Mobile without landing before setting a course for the return leg to Montgomery.

Shortly after midnight, the formation arrived over Mobile and adjusted the course for Montgomery. Approaching the small rural community of Atmore, Alabama, the formation encountered a layer of haze that obscured an area of rain showers. Because of the reduced visibility, several of the inexperienced cadets became disorientated and began to have trouble maintaining control of their aircraft. Desperately seeking improved weather conditions, the student aviators attempted to reverse course to return to Mobile. Within minutes, the combination of inadequate navigational equipment and limited pilot

Vultee BT-13 aircraft were utilized in the basic flight training program at Gunter Field during the Second World War. *AFHRA.*

experience resulted in aircraft becoming scattered in multiple directions. As the minutes stretched into hours, aircraft began running out of fuel as the pilot trainees attempted to find safe places to land. Of the thirty-five aircraft that departed earlier in the evening, only five would return to land safely at Gunter Field.

The remaining members of the flight met varying fates. The seven fatalities occurred in crashes in the vicinity of the town of Atmore. One student landed safely in the same area, while two others utilized their parachutes to survive that tragic night. The remaining cadets landed their aircraft at

Fatally injured during the predawn hours of May 21, 1942, Royal Air Force cadet Michael Peachell was buried at the Oakwood Cemetery Annex in Montgomery.

airfields in Crestview and Pensacola, Florida, and Mobile, Greenville and Evergreen, Alabama.

In times of war, loss of life often extends beyond the field of battle, extinguishing the hopes and dreams of those who selflessly give their lives in a foreign land far from home. In a tranquil corner of the annex of Oakwood Cemetery in Montgomery, seventy-eight headstones will forever stand as a reminder of the sacrifice of those who can never return home. Words etched into the face of the granite headstones represent a life lost, a solemn reminder that "This quiet corner of a distant foreign field shall be forever England."

TWELVE O'CLOCK HIGH OVER ALABAMA

Premiered in Los Angeles in December 1949, the Twentieth Century Fox production *Twelve O'Clock High* was nominated for four Academy Awards and would be selected as one of the Best 1,000 Motion Pictures of all time by the *New York Times*.

Based on the 1948 novel written by Sy Bartlett and Bernie Lay Jr., a book that recounted the experiences of the authors during their service with the 8th Air Force in England during the Second World War, the title of the film refers to the practice of identifying the positions of attacking enemy aircraft by reference to an imaginary clock face, with the outline of the bomber aircraft as the center of the dial. The film would eventually become required viewing for all United States military service academies as a teaching example for situational leadership theory. The film was also used in civilian applications relating to the study of leadership and management principles.

The plot of the film is based on the experiences of the fictional 908th Bomb Group that operated from Archbury airfield in England, known as a hard-luck group because of an excessive loss rate of aircraft and personnel during daylight bombing missions over Germany. Brigadier General Frank Savage, played by Gregory Peck, is appointed commanding officer of the bomb group to improve morale and operational performance. A stern disciplinarian, Savage initially alienates the men under his command as he attempts to correct the perception that problems experienced by the group are due solely to bad luck.

The movie was originally scheduled to be filmed in Santa Barbara, California, but producers determined the site to be unsuitable because the surrounding terrain did not closely resemble the English countryside. To identify a more appropriate location for filming, director Henry King arranged with the chief of staff of the air force to appoint Colonel John de Russy as technical advisor to the project. Stationed at Maxwell Air Force Base in Montgomery, de Russy was assigned to the Air Command and Staff College as an instructor. During his association with the production of *Twelve O'Clock High*, Colonel de Russy would coordinate military support for the film from his office on the base.

Initially, four locations were considered for filming scenes involving Boeing B-17 Flying Fortress bombardment aircraft to be used in the movie. However, de Russy suggested the search be limited to sites in Alabama and Florida because of the availability of B-17 aircraft that could be made available for the movie.

In March 1949, King arrived at Maxwell Air Force Base to confer with de Russy. After touring Eglin Air Force Base in Florida, they visited the Ozark Army Air Field in Alabama, a former training field had had been deactivated after the war. Because the facility was not being utilized as an active airfield, the site provided an ideal location for filming the takeoff and landing scenes of the B-17 aircraft. The surrounding terrain also shared a striking similarity to the English countryside, a consideration that allowed for filming additional footage of the aircraft in flight.

The field at Ozark also proved advantageous because of the World War II–era asphalt runways. During the Second World War, American and British airfields maintained dark-colored runways to make the bases more difficult for the enemy to locate from the air. Modern runways at other bases in the United States were constructed using concrete of a lighter color. To maintain an accurate and authentic look, all scenes involving takeoff and landing operations were filmed at the Ozark location.

For the aerial footage, the air force loaned Twentieth Century Fox twelve Boeing B-17 Flying Fortress aircraft, complete with flight and ground support crews. Eight of the aircraft were acquired from Eglin Air Force Base, with the remaining four on loan from Brookley Air Force Base in Mobile. The aircraft provided by Brookley Air Force Base had previously been utilized as cloud-sampling drones during Operation Crossroads, the postwar testing of atomic bombs at Bikini Atoll in the Marshall Islands. Even though the aircraft still retained evidence of residual radiation, the effects were determined to be negligible for the short periods of time the aircraft were to be used.

For the scenes filmed at the Ozark field, the studio chartered a Delta Airlines Douglas DC-4 four-engine civilian airliner to transport actor Gregory Peck and the cast and crew from the primary filming location at Eglin Air Force Base. If the filming was scheduled for early in the day, motel rooms in Enterprise and Ozark would be reserved to accommodate the actors and camera crew.

One of the most dramatic and memorable scenes in the movie involved a battle-damaged B-17 returning to land following a mission over Germany. The script called for the aircraft to land with the landing gear retracted, sliding to a stop between two tents that had been erected in a grassy area adjacent to one of the runways. Although the air force allowed its personnel to operate the large bombers in aerial formations, military personnel were prohibited from participating in the crash scene. The studio retained legendary Hollywood stunt pilot Paul Mantz to perform the dangerous stunt.

Actor Gregory Peck always attracted adoring fans during the filming of the movie *Twelve O'Clock High*. *AFHRA*.

The opening crash scene of the movie *Twelve O'Clock High* was filmed at the Ozark Army Air Field. *ALAMY*.

The B-17 selected by de Russy for the crash scene was one of the Bikini drones supplied by Brookley Air Force Base that was deemed expendable. In utilizing the aircraft for the crash sequence, the studio would be responsible for costs associated with salvage of the wreckage and return of the aircraft to a site designated by the commanding officer of Brookley Air Force Base.

There was no room for error in filming the crash scene, as it was doubtful the air force would provide another aircraft for the studio to destroy. In preparation for the scene, the B-17 was serviced with a minimum amount of fuel to minimize the chance of fire. A metal rod was welded across the engine controls on the flight deck to allow Mantz to turn off the ignition to all four engines as soon as the aircraft touched down. Established on the final approach for landing at an indicated airspeed of 110 miles per hour, Mantz maneuvered the thirty-eight-thousand-pound aircraft, christened the *Eager Beaver*, to a touchdown beside the runway. Skidding along the grass, Mantz managed to steer the giant aircraft by selective use of the brakes after discovering that even though the landing gear was retracted, enough of the two main wheels remained exposed below the wings to offer some directional control. Paul Mantz collected a fee of $1,500 for what has been described as one of the greatest aerial sequences ever produced for a motion picture.

Considered one of the greatest of the World War II–era films, *Twelve O'Clock High* was selected for preservation in the U.S. National Film Registry by the Library of Congress in 1998 as being culturally, historically and aesthetically relevant. For a brief period in 1949, the historical accuracy of the film was demonstrated daily for the residents of Ozark as a formation of Boeing B-17 aircraft departed each morning on their assigned mission. As the people of the town searched overhead to identify the source of the roar of the engines, they only had to look "Twelve o'Clock High."

A Hangar for Alabama College

In June 1930, the Olmsted Brothers architectural firm, known for its designs of Central Park in New York and the Biltmore Estate in Asheville, North Carolina, submitted a proposal to the president of Alabama College (present-day University of Montevallo) for the future development of that institution. The proposal included construction of a massive physical education complex to promote health and recreation of the students, factors that an editorial in the campus newspaper, the *Alabamian*, endorsed as being an essential element of a well-rounded college education.

The massive facility would be the largest of any building in the state educational system, extending fourteen feet longer than an average city block. One wing of the building would include a large gymnasium, while the opposite wing consisted of a swimming pool of graduated depth. Office space, classrooms and shower facilities were also included in the design. Dedication of the site of the proposed $200,000 structure would coincide with the October 1930 Founder's Day celebration.

With considerable fanfare, the site was cleared and ground broken for the physical education facility, slated to be named for Governor Bibb Graves. However, the faculty and student body were soon shocked and disappointed to learn that the project had been abruptly halted because of the devastating effects of the fiscal crisis that gripped the national economy, an event that severely curtailed financial assistance for campus construction projects. Alabama College administrators began a frantic search to identify other sources of funding to build the facility slated to become the centerpiece of the future development of the college.

Although financial assistance for construction of a gymnasium was not available, officials of the college became aware that funding for other types of structures could be secured through the federal Civil Works Administration (CWA). Established during the administration of President Franklin Delano Roosevelt, the CWA and its successor, the Works Progress Administration, worked in cooperation with state and local governments to create jobs for workers adversely affected by the financial crisis.

The focus of CWA projects would periodically change based on needs identified in various parts of the country. In 1935, administrators of the CWA began focusing their efforts on federal, state and local infrastructure projects. This mandate not only included funding for highways, roads and other means of surface transportation but also identified airports as a national priority. Because funding was not available for a physical education building, administrators of Alabama College submitted a request to the CWA for financial assistance to construct a hangar and runway to serve a dual purpose as an airport and physical education facility.

Once the project was approved, construction of the hangar began on March 23, 1935, with the $16,209.08 cost to be provided by the federal government. Concurrent with construction of the hangar, workers began grading an area for a runway, 2,200 feet in length and 300 feet in width. Because the runway would be located in the area originally designated as an athletic field, college administrators believed that the work would constitute a permanent improvement of great value that would accommodate various types of athletic events without interfering with its use as an airport. The sod surface of the runway proved to be ideal for various outdoor sports such as tennis, volleyball and archery.

From the outset, the plan to utilize the hangar structure and landing field for athletic purposes was obvious. During construction of the facility, representatives of the college continued to negotiate with federal officials to enter into an agreement to utilize the hangar and runway for the school's physical education curriculum. Administrators remained confident that the college would eventually be allowed to convert the runway and hangar into the physical education facility they desired.

Even though the runway and hangar were primarily used for physical education classes, pilots would occasionally land their aircraft on campus. In an article published in the August 8, 1935 *Union Banner* newspaper, W.M. Wyatt wrote, "We took off from the Clanton Airport about five o'clock and

Administrators of Alabama College obtained funds to construct an airplane hangar to be used as a gymnasium. *University of Montevallo Archives.*

in seventeen minutes were on the ground at the Montevallo airport, cool as a cucumber and talking with friends about the wonderful adventure."

By 1938, with the approval of federal officials, the conversion of the hangar into a much-needed fieldhouse had been completed. A substantial addition to the front of the building was added that, combined with the original floor space of the former hangar, created an area large enough to install a hardwood court adaptable for indoor athletics. A dance studio was later constructed at the rear of the building.

Although the landing field and hangar were never fully utilized for aviation purposes, the facility did continue to attract aircraft. The number of pilots utilizing the athletic field for takeoffs and landings became so frequent that by 1946 it had become necessary for the school to place an item on the front page of the *Montevallo Times* in which school administrators announced that no part of the college campus or its surrounding property could be used as a landing field for publicly or privately owned aircraft.

Since 1935, the hangar of Alabama College has hosted basketball games, volleyball matches, intramural sports and dance rehearsals. The building has also been the site of dances, music recitals and concerts. In the summer of 2020, the building underwent another significant transformation when the University of Montevallo Board of Trustees voted to rename Bibb Graves Hall because of the former governor's support of racial segregation. Today,

For almost a century, the converted aircraft hangar has continued to be utilized by students at the University of Montevallo.

the simple informational sign identifies the building only as the Old Gym. The former runway is covered in asphalt, serving its new role as an access road and parking lot for the automobiles of the faculty and students.

The hangar that was never a hangar still stands on the campus of the University of Montevallo. Erected during the most severe economic crisis in American history, the building has accommodated generations of students who have passed through its doors. Although this historic structure was never utilized for its intended function, the storage of aircraft, the building has served a noble purpose for more than eight decades by providing shelter for those students participating in physical education activities, an essential element of a well-rounded college education.

USS *BIRMINGHAM*

On November 14, 1910, civilian aviator Eugene Ely achieved the first successful takeoff of an airplane from the deck of a U.S. Navy ship using a Curtiss Model D biplane. The ship, the USS *Birmingham*, a Chester Class cruiser named for the largest city in Alabama, was modified with a wooden platform eighty feet in length that was erected on the bow of the ship. Ely barely succeeded in the attempt as his Curtiss pusher-type airplane rolled off the edge of the platform and briefly skipped off the water before becoming airborne. Ely managed to remain airborne and landed his machine on the nearest land after flying about two miles. The flight that originated on the deck of the USS *Birmingham* has been described as the birth of naval aviation.

LINDBERGH COMES TO ALABAMA

In May 1927, twenty-five-year-old airmail pilot Charles Lindbergh earned world acclaim by being the first to successfully cross the Atlantic Ocean by airplane during his historic nonstop flight from New York to Paris, France. Four years before achieving this remarkable feat, Lindbergh landed in Montgomery, Alabama, at the conclusion of his first solo cross-country flight by airplane, taking the first step in his journey to an illustrious aviation career.

In May 1923, the young aviator made his way from Nebraska to Americus, Georgia, to purchase a military surplus Curtiss JN-4 "Jenny" training aircraft. After finalizing the purchase, Lindbergh completed his first solo flight at the landing field in Americus. Before returning to Nebraska in his newly acquired machine, he set out for Montgomery to have the radiator of the water-cooled engine of the "Jenny" repaired by mechanics at Maxwell Field. Lindbergh's flight from Americus to Montgomery represents the first time the aviator, who would soon become known around the world as the "Lone Eagle," piloted a flight from one airport to another by himself.

Lindbergh returned to Alabama in October 1927 during an aerial tour of the United States following his flight from New York to Paris. After landing at Roberts Field in Birmingham, more than 200,000 residents greeted the aviator during a parade through downtown Birmingham.

I SAW THE LIGHT

In *Hank Williams: The Biography*, author Colin Escott described how the country music legend was inspired by an Alabama airport to compose one of his most memorable gospel recordings. In January 1947, Williams and members of his Drifting Cowboys band were returning home to Montgomery following a performance at a popular nightspot in Fort Deposit, Alabama. Traveling along U.S. Highway 31 late that winter evening, Lillie Williams, mother of the entertainer, was driving the car while Hank and members of his band slept. Having frequently traveled the route, she knew that they were nearing home when she saw the sweeping light beam of the navigation beacon of the Montgomery Municipal Airport, a visual aid used by pilots to locate the airfield at night. Knowing that it would take time to rouse Hank, Lillie nudged her son and stated, "Hank, wake up, we are nearly home. I just saw the light." By the time the group arrived in Montgomery, Hank Williams had penned the words of the gospel melody "I Saw the Light."

Released in September 1948, "I Saw the Light" became one of the most recognized and popular songs performed and recorded by Hank Williams. In 2005, the song inspired by the lighted navigation beacon of an Alabama airport was ranked first in Country Music Television's Twenty Greatest Songs of Faith.

ALABAMA AVIATORS

Throughout the history of powered flight, Alabama aviators have remained at the forefront of the evolution of aviation and have made significant contributions to the advancement of aeronautics both in and beyond the state of Alabama.

AIR FORCE ONE: THE ALABAMA CONNECTION

With a wink from the President of the United States and the realization that I had been in the midst of the small talk of the leaders of the United States of America, I was a long way from that Alabama cotton patch.
—James U. Cross

It is difficult to envision the cotton patches and steel mills of Depression-era Alabama as being fertile ground for anything more than an opportunity for survival for during one of the most challenging financial environments in the history of the United States. Yet these humble surroundings would produce two aviators whose professional careers would converge on the flight deck of the most recognizable aircraft in the world during an extraordinary period in American history.

James Barney Swindal was born on August 18, 1917, in the small central Alabama mining town of West Blockton. As the effects of the financial depression of 1929 created havoc on the national economy, the Swindal family moved to the Tarrant community near Birmingham in search of financial security. Swindal enrolled at Jefferson County High School, where he became a versatile athlete, participating in a variety of sports. After graduation, he remained in Tarrant working in various jobs, including two years as a pipe inspector and crane operator for the National Cast Iron Pipe Company.

The December 7, 1941 attack by the Imperial Japanese Navy on the U.S. Naval Base at Pearl Harbor in the Hawaiian Territory drew the United States into a second world conflict. The declaration of war against Japan, Germany and Italy significantly affected the lives of James Swindal and thousands of young men of his generation. In February 1942, Swindal enlisted as an aviation cadet in the Army Air Forces at Maxwell Field in Montgomery.

After earning his wings as a military aviator, Second Lieutenant Swindal served in the China-Burma-India Theater of Operations, flying Curtis C-46 cargo aircraft over the Himalayan Mountains. Nicknamed "the Hump" by allied pilots, the route was utilized to supply Chinese military forces in their struggle against the Imperial Japanese Army. It was considered the most dangerous of any military airlift operation, and more than 600 aircraft and 1,000 pilots were lost to accidents along the perilous 530-mile route. In a news article describing the hazards of the airlift operation, CBS News correspondent Eric Sevareid reported, "Pilots could plot their course to China by the line of smoking wrecks scattered along the hillsides." Because of the numerous accident sites, reporters soon began referring to the route as the "Aluminum Trail." From April to December 1944, Swindal completed eighty-five missions flying over the Hump.

Swindal's participation in military airlift missions would not end with the conclusion of the Second World War. During the Berlin Crisis (1948–49) in which the Soviet Union established a blockade to prevent ground access to the city, James Swindal flew fifty-one humanitarian missions to supply the people of Berlin with food and provisions. Extended periods of inclement weather, rudimentary navigation aids, inadequate airfield facilities and harassment by Soviet fighter aircraft posed a constant threat to aviators operating into the divided capital of the German republic.

In June 1951, Swindal transferred to the newly established 1254th Air Transport Squadron. Recognizing the need to provide secure aerial transportation for the president and other government dignitaries, the air force established a team of highly experienced personnel to operate and maintain a fleet of modified transport aircraft to complete these specialized missions. Initially operating from the Washington National Airport, the

1254th Air Transport Squadron was be reassigned to Andrews Air Force Base as the 89th Airlift Wing.

As one of the most experienced pilots serving in the 89th Airlift Wing, Swindal was instrumental in the transition of presidential air travel into the jet age by coordinating the development and delivery of the VC-137C, a highly modified civilian Boeing 707 four-engine aircraft designated SAM 26000, to replace the older propeller-driven transports. Selected as pilot for president-elect John Fitzgerald Kennedy following the 1960 presidential election, Colonel James Swindal was officially appointed as the pilot of Air Force One in January 1961.

During his tenure as command pilot of Air Force One, Swindal participated in several historic events. In June 1963, President Kennedy traveled to Berlin, the first trip for Swindal into that beleaguered city since participating in the postwar airlift. Standing at the Brandenburg Gate, Kennedy spoke to more than 200,000 residents of the divided city. He concluded his remarks with the words that would resonate in democracies around the world: "All free men, wherever they may live, are citizens of Berlin, and, therefore, as a free man, I take pride in the words '*Ich bin ein Berliner*' ('I am a Berliner')."

Swindal would serve as the presidential pilot during one of the most dangerous periods of escalating tensions between the United States and Russia during the Cold War: the thirteen days of the Cuban Missile Crisis in October 1962 that brought the world to the brink of nuclear conflict. However, the career of James Swindal will forever be associated with the historic flight from Love Field in Dallas to Washington, D.C., on November 22, 1963, set into motion by three shots fired from the sixth floor of the Texas School Book Depository.

Originally scheduled to fly President Kennedy to Bergstrom Air Force Base in Austin following a speech at the Dallas Trade Mart, Swindal and copilot Lewis Hanson were completing their preflight tasks in preparation for the brief flight. As Swindal sat in the cockpit of Air Force One monitoring radio transmissions of Secret Service agents accompanying the presidential motorcade, he heard agent Roy Kellerman suddenly transmit an ominous message: "Lancer [the codename for the president] is hurt. It looks bad. We have to get to a hospital."

At 12:50 p.m., Colonel Swindal received an urgent message from General Godfrey McHugh, top military aide to the president, to immediately fuel the aircraft and file a flight plan for Andrews Air Force Base. Swindal would learn of the death of the president only when he turned on the

In January 1961, James Barney Swindal was appointed by President John F. Kennedy as command pilot of Air Force One. *James Swindal.*

television in the presidential compartment of the aircraft. By order of succession mandated by the Constitution, Vice President Lyndon Johnson had become commander-in-chief.

After learning that Air Force One would be used to transport the body of President Kennedy back to Washington, Swindal quickly decided that neither protocol nor his personal feelings would allow the casket to be placed in the cargo compartment of the aircraft. He began preparations to make room in the passenger cabin to accommodate the fallen president for what would be his last flight on Air Force One. When the hearse carrying the president's body arrived, Swindal stood at attention at the base of the portable stairs used to access the aircraft. As the casket was carried onboard, his salute not only represented a professional demonstration of respect for the office but also a personal tribute to President Kennedy.

In the midsection of the aircraft, a group of twenty-seven people that included public officials, Secret Service agents and members of the press were tightly packed into the small presidential stateroom to witness the historic transfer of executive power as Lyndon Johnson repeated the oath of office, becoming the thirty-sixth president of the United States.

Preparing for departure, Colonel Swindal anticipated an air traffic control clearance that would include a route defined by a specific course and altitude for the trip to Washington. However, contacting ground controllers in Dallas, Swindal acknowledged one of the most unique air traffic control clearances in aviation history: "Air Force One, taxi to runway three-one right, cleared to Andrews Air Force Base by any route, any altitude." At 2:47 p.m. Central Standard Time, SAM 26000, codename Angel, lifted off the runway bound for Washington, D.C. During thirty years of subsequent service to five presidents, the aircraft would never again fly as high or as fast than it did on that day.

Although Swindal would never again carry John F. Kennedy aboard Air Force One, he would command one last flight to honor the former president. On November 25, 1963, as Kennedy was laid to rest at Arlington Cemetery, Swindal piloted SAM 26000 over the cemetery in a final salute. Surrounding Air Force One, a group of military fighter aircraft formed an

Colonel Swindal (*second from right*) and the support crew of Special Air Missions 26000, the aircraft designated as Air Force One.

inverted V formation, the last slot of the apex of the formation vacant, the symbol of a fallen flyer.

On the day of the assassination, Major James Cross was working in his office at Andrews Air Force Base. In 1961, three years after becoming a member of the Special Air Missions Wing, Major Cross became the pilot for Vice President Lyndon Johnson. In his autobiography *Around the World with LBJ*, Cross recalled, "The assassination of President John F. Kennedy changed Lyndon Johnson's life dramatically and forever. It changed mine too."

James Underwood Cross was born on April 25, 1925, in the Pleasant Home community of rural Covington County, Alabama. His father was employed by a lumber company as an operator of a pump station that supplied water from a nearby creek to steam locomotives used to transport harvested timber to sawmills and lumber yards. Following graduation from high school in June 1943, Cross enlisted as an aviation cadet in the Army Air Forces to begin flight training to develop the skills that would serve him for the remainder of his military career.

After being commissioned as a second lieutenant, Cross was assigned to the China-Burma-India Theater. Like James Swindal, Cross piloted Curtis C-46 Commando aircraft across the Himalayan Mountains. After completing his tour of duty in February 1946, Cross enrolled as a student at the Alabama Polytechnic Institute in Auburn. In October 1948, he was recalled to active duty with the onset of the Berlin Crisis. Cross was initially assigned to an aviation transport squadron at Clark Air Force Base in the Philippines. Electing to continue his career as a military aviator, he applied to the elite Special Air Missions group, whose motto, *Experto Crede*, proclaims "Trust those with experience."

Two weeks after Lyndon Johnson became president, James Cross received a call from the Oval Office. Johnson directed Cross to get qualified on the big jet. Initially, he would serve as copilot to Colonel Swindal until fully qualified to take command. For the next two years, James Swindal and James Cross, two military aviators from Alabama, would command the most recognizable aircraft while transporting the most powerful leader in the world. Cross recalled Johnson being the ultimate back-seat pilot, frequently ordering last-minute changes to schedules and itineraries. According to Cross, the president did not care about scheduling protocols when it came time for him to fly somewhere. He wanted to go, and he wanted to go immediately.

In July 1965, Lyndon Johnson nominated Cross to serve in the unprecedented position of Armed Forces aide and director of the White

President Lyndon Johnson in the cockpit of Air Force One with Command Pilot James Underwood Cross. *James U. Cross.*

House Military Office. Simultaneously, he was promoted to the rank of lieutenant colonel and assigned as command pilot of Air Force One, becoming the only pilot in the history of Air Force One to have one foot in the cockpit and the other in the inner circle of the White House. The Secret Service assigned Cross the codename Sawdust because he was a country boy from a sawmill town in the piney woods of south Alabama who never lost his backwoods drawl.

In December 1967, Colonel James Cross became the first presidential pilot to fly a United States president into a foreign war zone since Franklin Roosevelt reviewed American troops in Casablanca during the Second World War. The trip was originally planned as a goodwill tour that included stops in New Zealand, Australia, the Philippines and South Korea. Unknown to Cross, the trip would also include an unscheduled and unpublicized stop to visit troops in Southeast Asia.

During the two-day visit to the Philippines, President Johnson met with General William Westmoreland, commander of United States military forces in Vietnam. To improve morale among the troops, Johnson was encouraged to visit an American base in Vietnam before resuming his tour.

Command Pilot James Underwood Cross being observed by one of President Lyndon Johnson's pet beagles during a flight on Air Force One. *James U. Cross.*

The military air base at Cam Ranh Bay was selected for the presidential visit not only because it functioned as a major logistical and convalescent center for all branches of the United States military but also because it afforded a high degree of security.

With only minimal time for preparation, Cross and his crew departed the Philippines for Vietnam. Upon landing, Air Force One was greeted by seven thousand soldiers assembled for his arrival. A reporter for *Newsweek* later wrote that the president moved through Cam Ranh Bay like a locomotive, pressing flesh, yelling encouragement and having the time of his life. Air Force One returned to Andrews Air Force Base outside of Washington during the early morning hours of Christmas Eve. During the four-day junket, the aircraft flew fifty-nine hours and covered 26,959 miles, with landings in seven countries and territories. During the flight, Johnson became the first president of the United States to circumnavigate the globe by air.

In March 1968, during a televised national address on the war in Vietnam, Lyndon Johnson shocked the world with an unexpected announcement that he would not seek and would not accept the nomination of the Democratic Party for a second term as president. Although James Cross realized that his days as a presidential pilot were coming to an end, he did not anticipate that his service to Lyndon Johnson would continue after the president left office.

Following a brief tour of duty as a reconnaissance pilot in Vietnam, Cross served as wing commander of the 75th Tactical Reconnaissance Wing, Bergstrom Air Force Base, until his retirement in April 1971. Like James Swindal before him, Cross was called on to perform one final act of loyalty to the president he served. As custodian of the official funeral plan for Lyndon Johnson, Cross supervised the burial of his former commander-in-chief on January 25, 1973, at the Johnson Family Cemetery in Stonewall, Texas.

Brigadier General James Underwood Cross lived the remainder of his life on his cattle farm in Gatesville, Texas. The announcement of his death on July 11, 2015, was made by Lyndon Nugent, a grandson of the former president. His mentor on Air Force One, James Barney Swindal, retired from military service in 1971 as a colonel stationed at Patrick Air Force Base in Florida. He died of heart failure on April 25, 2005, at Cocoa Beach, Florida, and was buried at Arlington Cemetery only a short distance from the president he served.

The tragic death of President John F. Kennedy changed the lives of Alabamians James Swindal and James Cross dramatically and forever. As the pilots of Air Force One, these aviators transported the world's most powerful leader, on the world's most recognizable aircraft, during one of the most tumultuous periods in history. Throughout their careers, both men devoted their lives to their country and to the presidents they served. Like the eternal flame that illuminates the grave of John F. Kennedy at Arlington Cemetery, the memory of the patriotism, dedication and devotion of these Alabama aviators will never be extinguished.

The Chief and Mrs. Roosevelt

In an April 1939 *Collier's* magazine article, First Lady Eleanor Roosevelt wrote, "I enjoy flying because I see the country in a different way." Referred to by the media as "America's Flying First Lady" because of her frequent air travel, Roosevelt penned the article "Flying Is Fun" to convince the public that aircraft represented a safe and efficient means of transportation. Two years later, Eleanor Roosevelt's fondness for aviation and the opportunity it afforded her to see the country in a different way would bring about one of the most extraordinary events in the history of aviation in Alabama.

In October 1939, Tuskegee Institute became one of nine colleges and universities in Alabama to receive approval from the Civil Aeronautics Authority, predecessor the Federal Aviation Administration, to participate in the Civilian Pilot Training (CPT) Program. Created prior to the Second World War to provide flight training to civilian aviators in preparation for military service in the event of a national emergency, the program was established in response to the potential for war in Europe. Inauguration of the flight training program at Tuskegee would form the foundation for the training of Black aviators for service in the United States military.

Students participating in the CPT program at Tuskegee Institute received ground training on campus. Because the town of Tuskegee did not operate a municipal landing field approved by the Civil Aeronautics Authority, students were required to travel by bus to the Montgomery Municipal Airport for flight training. The eighty-mile round trip to Montgomery created immediate problems because students had to spend more than six hours away from campus to complete one thirty-minute training flight.

Construction of a landing field convenient to campus became crucial to the success of the training program. As an interim solution, G.L. Washington, director of the Department of Mechanical Industries at the university, proposed that flight training activities be relocated to Kennedy Field, a privately owned flying field located six miles south of Tuskegee on the Union Springs Highway. The fifty-five-acre site included two sod runways, the longest being 1,800 feet in length, and a small hangar. The field was operated by local aviator Stanley Kennedy, who agreed to transfer the lease to Tuskegee Institute on the condition that he would be allowed access for his personal flying activities.

Following an inspection by officials of the Civil Aeronautics Authority, Tuskegee Institute received approval to initiate flight training activities at Kennedy Field after required improvements were completed. Characteristic of the tradition of Tuskegee Institute, students volunteered to make the necessary improvements. Under the supervision of school instructors, students cut trees, graded the runway, erected a hangar and built a fuel depot and flight operations building. In February 1940, Kennedy Field was approved for CPT operations.

Although a more convenient flying field was now available, G.L. Washington and Tuskegee Institute president F.D. Patterson agreed that the success of aviation training at the school would be dependent on the development of a permanent facility. In addition to identifying a suitable site, Patterson faced the formidable challenge of securing the funding necessary

First Lady Eleanor Roosevelt and Charles Alfred "Chief" Anderson prepare for an aerial tour of the Tuskegee Institute campus. *AFHRA*.

for construction of the airfield. After making several unsuccessful attempts to arrange financing, Patterson approached the Julius Rosenwald Foundation, a philanthropic organization created by the president of the Sears, Roebuck and Company, to support public education for Black Americans. One of the more prominent trustees of the foundation was Eleanor Roosevelt, wife of President Franklin Roosevelt.

Because the board of the Julius Rosenwald Foundation was slated to meet in Tuskegee in March 1941, an air show was organized at Kennedy Field for members of the trustee board. During the demonstration, CPT students would conduct formation flights and perform aerobatics. Chief Flight Instructor Charles Alfred "Chief" Anderson recalled Mrs. Roosevelt stating that she had been told that Black people did not have the ability to operate aircraft. As she observed the activities, Roosevelt expressed her belief that the students appeared to be flying satisfactorily. The first lady then advised Anderson that she would find out for sure by going up in an airplane with him.

Her decision caused considerable concern among her personal aides and security detail, who considered contacting the president to try to stop her. However, once Eleanor Roosevelt made a decision, no amount of persuasion would dissuade her. Roosevelt proceeded to climb into the back seat of a Piper J-3 Cub, a two-seat, fabric-covered aircraft powered by a sixty-five-horsepower engine. Designed for basic pilot training, the aircraft was not equipped with navigation or communication equipment. Departing from one of the sod runways, Roosevelt and Anderson enjoyed a delightful thirty-minute flight over the campus and surrounding area. Roosevelt described her visit to Kennedy Field in her syndicated newspaper column, *My Day*.

Eleanor Roosevelt enjoyed flying because it allowed her to see the country in a different way. More important, her brief flight with Chief Anderson helped the American people to see their country in a different way. Within months of this historic flight, thirteen young men began primary flight training at the recently completed Moton Field, the new home of the 66th Army Air Forces Flying Training Detachment. These men became the first Black aviators to serve in the United States military. Before the end of the war, more than one thousand aviation cadets would follow in their footsteps, earning the honor and distinction of being Tuskegee Airmen.

Today, only the sound of vehicles along the Union Springs Highway disturbs the tranquility of a late afternoon at the former site of Kennedy Field. Covered by tall, slender pine trees that sway gracefully with the afternoon breeze, the former airfield on the Union Springs Highway has vanished, lost to the passage time. But the memory of Kennedy Field will forever remain ingrained in the history of aviation. During one afternoon in the fall of 1939, the field helped to teach the people of the United States to see their world in a different way.

A Lifetime Aloft

A popular bumper sticker that frequently adorns the vehicles of aviators reads, "God does not deduct from our allotted life span the time spent flying." For John Edward Long Jr. of Montgomery, recognized by the Guinness Book of World Records as having accumulated more flying time as a pilot than any other person in the history of aviation, that truism invokes a special meaning.

Born on November 10, 1915, in Montgomery, Alabama, Long took his first ride in an airplane in 1930 in a Ford Tri-Motor, the fifty-cent cost of the ride a gift from his grandmother. At the age of seventeen, he was able to afford his first flying lesson. Because of the ongoing financial depression, money for flying lessons was almost impossible to obtain. In 1933, Long began working at a local flying school by washing aircraft and doing odd jobs at the airport. Earning only thirty minutes of flying time for a week of work, progress was painfully slow. During the next three years, he was only able to accumulate one hour and forty minutes of instruction. In 1936, Ed Long finally realized his dream of becoming a pilot when he completed his first solo flight. His persistence was rewarded three years later when he completed the examination for certification as a pilot.

In 1940, Long enlisted in the Army Air Corps in the hope of being accepted into pilot training as an aviation cadet. However, because of his small stature, he did not meet the minimum height or weight requirements for training as a pilot. Fulfilling his desire to remain in aviation, Long completed training as an aircraft mechanic and crew chief on Consolidated B-24 Heavy Bombardment Aircraft, earning the rank of master sergeant.

After completing his military service, Long returned to Montgomery, where he found employment as a mechanic and pilot at the Norman Bridge Airport. In 1945, he became employed at Montgomery Aviation as a mechanic and pilot two weeks after the company was established.

In 1949, Montgomery Aviation was awarded a contract by the Alabama Power Company to conduct routine aerial inspections of the system of transmission lines that traversed the state. Within three years, Long would become the sole pilot responsible for conducting these flights, a position he would retain for forty-six years. During his tenure, Long rarely missed a flight. A typical mission involved operating at altitudes of less than two hundred feet above the ground, visually inspecting power poles and transmission lines for broken insulators, damaged poles and encroachments on the powerline right-of-way.

Long often flew as much as eight hours per day, five days each week. Unlike airline pilots, who accumulate flying hours in straight and level flight at high altitudes utilizing an autopilot and automated navigation systems, the Piper Super Cub aircraft used by Ed Long did not have an autopilot or sophisticated navigation system. Air conditioning was provided by the open side door of the aircraft. During the final ten years of his career, Long averaged more than 1,200 hours in the air each year.

John Edward Long Jr. is recognized by the Guinness Book of World Record as having accumulated more pilot time than any aviator in history. *AAHOF.*

Because he was able to complete his inspection flights in marginal weather conditions, Long never attempted to obtain certification to operate an aircraft solely by reference to flight instruments, as he considered it of little use in his work. He evaluated the weather by determining if distant hills were shrouded in clouds. If not, he could complete the flight safely.

In 1989, having accumulated 52,929 hours in the air, John Edward Long Jr. surpassed the record previously held by Max Conrad in accumulating more time as a pilot than any person in history. He would set a new world record with each flight until June 21, 1999, when he made the final entry into the last of his fourteen logbooks. On that day, John Edward Long Jr. established a world record of 64,397 hours in the air, more than seven years of his life spent in the skies over his home state of Alabama.

The increasing utilization of unpiloted aerial vehicles to conduct airborne activities, previously the sole domain of aircraft, will relegate many of these traditional aerial services to the pages of aviation history. For future generations, the world record of more than seven years aloft established by John Edward Long Jr. will be extremely difficult, if not impossible, to surpass and will continue to stand as an enduring testament to an Alabama aviator who devoted his life and allotted time on earth to the profession he loved.

JESSE FOLMAR, MARINE AVIATOR

On September 10, 1952, during one of the most intense periods of aerial combat of the Korean conflict, U.S. Marine Corps aviator Jesse Folmar of Montgomery would earn the Silver Star decoration for conspicuous gallantry against enemy aggressor forces when he became the first pilot of a propeller-driven aircraft to destroy an enemy jet fighter during aerial combat.

Approaching the coast of North Korea, the two-aircraft formation of Vought F4U Corsairs led by Folmar was attacked by eight Russian MiG-15 fighter jets. Folmar immediately began defensive maneuvers to evade the enemy attack. Aggressively maneuvering his aircraft, Folmar skillfully fired his 20mm cannon at one of the hostile aircraft as it streaked past his Corsair. The enemy aircraft burst into flames, forcing its pilot to escape by parachute before it impacted into the ocean below.

The remaining enemy fighters quickly reformed for a second attack. Facing overwhelming odds, Folmar's aircraft was severely damaged in the ensuing engagement, forcing him to parachute to safety. Landing in the

Marine Corps aviator Jesse Folmar of Montgomery became the first American credited with the destruction of a jet fighter while flying a piston-powered aircraft. *AAHOF.*

ocean, Folmar was quickly recovered by an amphibious rescue aircraft. Forty years after this historic engagement, military sources revealed that the pilot of the enemy aircraft destroyed by Jesse Folmar was a member of the Russian air force.

Jesse Gregory Folmar retired from active duty in 1961 after faithfully serving the people of the United States for twenty-three years. Following his death in July 2004, he was buried at the Pine Rest Cemetery in Foley, Alabama.

THE LAST ACE

Born on July 10, 1896, in Suggsville, Alabama, Charles Rudolph D'Olive enlisted in the Aviation Section of the U.S. Army Signal Corps on April 28, 1917, in Memphis, Tennessee, where he became a member of the first class of American pilots to be trained for service in the First World War. Upon completion of primary and advanced flight training, D'Olive was assigned to the 93rd Pursuit Squadron near Vaucouleures, France.

On September 12, 1918, Lieutenant D'Olive achieved the first victory for the 93rd Pursuit Squadron when he destroyed a German Fokker D-VII aircraft during aerial combat. The next day, D'Olive engaged five hostile aircraft during a routine patrol. He would be awarded the Distinguished Service Cross for extraordinary heroism by destroying three of the enemy aircraft during the subsequent aerial battle. Five days later, D'Olive destroyed another enemy aircraft to achieve a total of five aerial victories in a seven-day period. The victory should have earned him the distinction of being an Ace fighter pilot, a designation reserved for military aviators credited with five aerial victories. Because of a clerical error, however, only two of the victories achieved during the engagement of September 13, 1918, were officially recorded, leaving D'Olive one victory short of the five required for official designation as an Ace.

In 1967, almost fifty years after the end of the First World War, D'Olive petitioned military officials to examine the discrepancy that existed among the citation for his Distinguished Service Cross medal and the official combat records of his former squadron. Following an extensive review, the fifth aerial victory was affirmed and the title of Ace bestowed on Charles Rudolph D'Olive, the last aviator of the First World War to achieve this distinction.

Charles Rudolph D'Olive of Suggsville, Alabama, was the last American aviator of the First World War to be designated a flying ace. *AAHOF.*

On October 1, 2016, a painting depicting the September 13, 1918 three-victory flight of Charles Rudolph D'Olive was unveiled at the National Museum of the United States Air Force in Dayton, Ohio—official recognition that will permanently preserve the historic achievement and distinguished military service of a remarkable Alabama aviator.

BIBLIOGRAPHY

Baime, A.J. *The Arsenal of Democracy: FDR, Detroit, and an Epic Quest to Arm an America at War.* Boston: Houghton Mifflin Harcourt, 2014.

Ball, T.H. *Clarke County Alabama and Its Surroundings.* Grove Hill, AL: Clarke County Historical Society, 1973.

Bell, Landon C. *The Old Free State: A Contribution to the History of Lunenburg County and Southside Virginia.* Vol. 2. Baltimore, MD: Clearfield Company, 1974.

Burden, Maria Schell. *The Life and Times of Robert G. Fowler.* Los Angeles: Borden Publishing Company, 1999.

Crofton, Ian. *In the Words of the Presidents.* London: Quercus Publishing, 2010.

Cross, James U. *Around the World With LBJ.* Austin: University of Texas Press, 2008.

Duffin, Allan T., and Paul Matheis. *The 12 o'Clock High Logbook.* Boalsburg, PA: BearManor Media, 2005.

Dwiggins, Don. *Hollywood Pilot: The Biography of Paul Mantz.* New York: Doubleday and Company Inc., 1967.

Escott, Colin. *Hank Williams: The Biography.* Boston: Little, Brown and Company, 1994.

Jakeman, Robert J. *The Divided Skies: Establishing Segregated Flight Training at Tuskegee, Alabama, 1934–942.* Tuscaloosa: University of Alabama Press, 1992.

Kane, Robert B. *So Far from Home: Royal Air Force and Free French Air Force Flight Training at Maxwell and Gunter Fields during World War II.* Montgomery, AL: NewSouth Books, 2016.

Klass, Phillip J. *UFOs Explained.* New York: Random House, 1974.

Manchester, William. *The Death of a President.* New York: Harper and Row, 1967.

Marty, John L., Jr. "The Steamship Airline." *Airways* 12, no. 5, issue 113 (July 2005): 53–57.

———. "The Steamship Airline." *Airways* 12, no. 6, issue 114 (August 2005): 55–59.

Newton, Wesley Phillips. "Military Bases." In *The Great War in the Heart of Dixie: Alabama during World War I.* Edited by Martin T. Oliff. Tuscaloosa: University of Alabama Press, 2008.

Perna, Albert F. *The Glider Gladiators of World War II.* Freeman, SD: Pine Hill Press, 1970.

Ronnie, Art. *Locklear: The Man Who Walked on Wings.* New York: A.S. Barnes and Company Inc., 1973.

Singleton, Billy J. "Air Force One: The Alabama Connection." *Alabama Heritage*, no. 139 (Winter 2021): 8–19.

———. "Alabama's First Ladies of Flight." *Alabama Heritage*, no. 146 (Fall 2022): 10–23.

———. "Dreams of Flying Machines." *Alabama Heritage*, no. 127 (Winter 2018): 32–43.

Wright, Orville. *How We Made the First Flight.* Reprint. Washington, D.C.: Federal Aviation Administration Office of Public Affairs, 1986.

Wynne, H. Hugh. *The Motion Picture Stunt Pilots and Hollywood's Classic Aviation Movies.* Missoula, MT: Pictorial Histories Publishing Company, 1987.

About the Author

B illy J. Singleton is a retired professional pilot and has been involved in the aviation industry for five decades. A native of Alabama, he earned a bachelor's degree from Troy University and a Master of Aeronautical Science degree from Embry-Riddle Aeronautical University. He has served as chair of the board of directors of the Alabama Aviation Hall of Fame, the Southern Museum of Flight and the National Soaring Safety Foundation. He is the author of six books, is a regular contributor to local, state and national publications and is a frequent speaker on topics relating to aviation history in Alabama.

Visit us at
www.historypress.com